One Man's Story

By
Freddie Lee Caldwell

ISBN-13: 978-1497523685

ISBN-10: 1497523680

Dedication:

This book is dedicated to the memory and the contribution of Denver C. Caldwell and his lovely wife Catherine Caldwell. These are the two people who started this segment of the Caldwell clan. Thank you Mama and Daddy from all of the members of this family that came after you.

One Man's Story

Table of Contents

Introduction

Today, across America, we are seeing men and women tell their life stories in book form. From these stories we get a feel for life in the United States of America. We learn what Americans believe, what we teach, and how we live.

We can read stories about people living on farms growing food for the world. We can read stories about people climbing mountains, fishing on boats, and piloting airplanes.

We can read stories about people working hard trying to make things better for themselves and their families. We can read stories about the dreams that came true as a result of hard work and perseverance.

This book is about one of those American men who has lived his entire life in this country, and considers himself a hard core American.

He was born and raised in Central Florida, and has spent his adult life in Upstate New York.

He served in the United States Armed Forces during the time of the draft and gave two years of his life in the defense of this nation.

This is one man's story!

The approach that will be used is to introduce you (the reader) to his family members, and recount some of his childhood memories. You will come to understand how this American views himself, and his membership in this society.

Through the words written in this book the reader will become familiar with this American's growing up, his educational process, his military experience, his work life, and some of the people who most influenced his human and social development.

We will look at his marriages and how they assisted in making him the person he is today.

This is the story of an African American male, now 67 years of age, and it will have the reader look at the American dream from his perspective. Hopefully one result of reading this book will be to spark a conversation about diversity, and its impact on all of America.

Hopefully this book will challenge the reader to perceive how our peoples' differences help to make America great.

The reader will be exposed to some of the opinions of this man on issues that Americans tend to avoid. It seems strange that the lists of subjects most Americans avoid talking about are the very ones that should be discussed in order for this country to become the great nation God intended it to be.

It has taken five years to develop and organize the information shared in this book. Many memories were recounted by his family members, fellow workers, and associates over a long period of time.

It has been said that you can learn a lot about a person by looking at their family members, the places they have been, and the things they have done. Hopefully this book will do that too!

This man was born in Sanford, Florida and reared in the South. He has lived his adult life in the North. This book will allow the reader to get to know him by taking a view of the life he lived in both places.

Three marriages, and assisting in upbringing eleven people (who are now adults), helped to formulate the person you are about to meet.

The reader will hopefully begin to see the uselessness of racial discrimination in the 21st Century. It may have had some use in maintaining the institution of slavery but serves no purpose today.

The reader will hopefully accept and understand that we human beings are 96% the same…..and those other four percentage points are of no consequence!

It is hoped that this book will spark that conversation, and we will all be better people because of it.

This is just one man's story much like many others, and I hope you enjoy getting to know him.

Chapter One

Family Members

I am Freddie Lee Caldwell, an African American male, 67 years of age, and in my third marriage. I have children that are biological, and those non-biological I helped to raise in my second and third marriages. All of these children mean something special to me.

I was born in Sanford, Florida, August 6, 1946. My father's name is Denver C. Caldwell. My mother's name is Catherine (Nelson) Caldwell.

I am the seventh of eight children (three boys and five girls). Six of my siblings were born to Denver and Catherine Caldwell.*

In this book I will write about my relationships with each member of my family, my relationship with my hometown, my school, some friends, and share some of my life experiences.

In sharing this information I hope you will begin to develop a picture of a person who loves life, loves to laugh and spend time with the people he loves, and cares about.

My father's family tree as I can best tell it???

Weldon Caldwell was a White land owner who lived in South Carolina in the 1850's. His wife's name was May Belle Caldwell. They had four children: two boys and two girls. May Belle died during child birth with the last child, a girl, so Mr. Weldon named her May Belle after her mother.

*My brother Horrest Caldwell (*Hot Stuff*) had a different mother.

Mr. Weldon owned twelve slaves. Two of the slaves were house slaves (husband and wife), and the rest were slaves that worked the fields, brought in the harvest from the fields, and tended the farm animals.

The two house slaves, Beth and William, helped Mr. Weldon raise his four children. They were all very close.

Beth and William, like most of the slaves of those times, carried the last name of their owner (Caldwell).

William and Beth had two sons of their own. Mr. Weldon named one Zimmerman and the other he named Nathan. All of the Caldwell slaves could read and write. Mr. Weldon thought his business would run much smoother if all of his slaves could read and write.

The only book available to learn to read from was the Holy Bible. Mr. Weldon and Mrs. May Belle taught all of the slaves to read and write. This was a family secret of course because it was against the law for anyone to teach slaves to read and write. For Whites the punishment was 10 years in prison, and death for a Black person.

After the Civil War, in the mid-1870s, Zimmerman became a traveling teacher and taught school in short bursts all over South Carolina, Georgia, Alabama, Mississippi, and Florida. Zimmerman taught in short bursts because when the word got around that Blacks were being taught to read and write the teacher would be hunted down, and killed.

Nathan became a preacher, and it is said he memorized the entire Bible.

Both Zimmerman and Nathan traveled all over the Southeastern United States teaching and preaching.

Those Caldwell men left babies everywhere they went. Zimmerman left one in Havana, Florida with Susie *"Coon"* McBride, and that is where Denver C. Caldwell came from!

My Father – Denver C. Caldwell

My father was born in Havana, Florida in 1909. He and my mother moved to Sanford, Florida because her family felt she could have done much better than my father.

My father was very dark-skinned, and my mother was much lighter ("high yellow" we call it in Florida). In the African American community in the early 1900s skin color was one of many issues that caused us problems.

My father is a descendant of Zimmerman Caldwell. Zimmerman was a traveling teacher from South Carolina. Zimmerman traveled and taught school throughout the Southeastern United States.

My father's grandmother was said to have been a full-blooded Native American. Her daughter, Susie McBride (nick-named "Coon"), was my father's mother.

My father was a strong disciplinarian, and ruled the home with a strong hand. He never worked for anyone. He was always self-employed. He became known as the "Snow-Cone Man."

He cleaned windows in peoples' homes and at store fronts, cut grass, trimmed hedges, and did all sorts of work.

He was also known as *"Sweet Man"* because he sold perfumes, cologne, women's wigs, and other personal and home care items. I know because he carried me with him if I was not in school.

His life principle was: *"There is a place for everything, and everything should be in its place."* My father used to say if you lived your life by this principle you would never have to clean up! He died in August of 1979.

In our home we all had a place at the dinner table. No one got their place confused because if you did, you would hear from the old man!

I remember when I was having trouble in school Daddy would help me with my reading skills. He chose not to use the school books; instead he made me read the Bible. He said that all the answers to man's issues were addressed in the Bible.

I remember each evening we would go into his bedroom and he would read a chapter from the Bible, and we would talk about it.

I would read a chapter and we would talk about it. We worked our way through the entire Bible.

I remember one morning as he was leaving for work he told me to wipe off his tools and put them away. He normally put his tools away himself but this day he needed to have something for me to do while he was working. My friends and I played around all day.

My mother told me several times to do what my father had requested. I said, "OK Mama," and kept on playing.

Late that afternoon I heard my father ringing the snow- cone bell on the way home. I had not wiped off the tools, nor had I put them away. I knew it was too late!

As he was coming into the driveway I was going into the garage to do the tools. He saw what was going on and said in a voice that I knew meant trouble: "Don't you put your hands on my devilish tools!" Oh he was cussing now! There was smoke coming out of his ears!

My mother was crying, and I was crying, because we both knew what was going to happen. He cleaned out his snow- cone cart, we had dinner, and he never said a word. Then when it was dark, and I could not see, he told me to go out into the garage, wipe off the tools, and put them away. He said I had all day of sunlight to do what he had asked, and sunlight is free!

I was not allowed to turn on the light. My mother shined the flashlight so that I could see. God bless my mother!

After the job was completed, and I went into the house, I got one of those *"Orange Grove Central Florida Ass Whippings."* That was just one of many over the years!

My father never gave me money: I always had to earn it. He would come home sometimes and tell me to go around to one of the neighbor's home and cut the grass. I would receive three dollars and that would be my allowance. He would sometimes send me to another person's home to do yard work for which I would get paid, and I could keep the money.

I also sold snow-cones on Sanford Avenue near our home. Working all day Saturday I could earn as much as $50.00.

This was in the early 1960s and that was a lot of money for a young man to earn. Daddy would take $45.00 and give me $5.00. That was my allowance.

Many times he would allow me to hold money for him. He said it was to teach me how to handle money. I would walk around with a one hundred dollar bill in my pocket. All I could do was show it off to my friends. He would say, "Boy give me that hundred, and keep this fifty." Of course I could not spend it but I could keep it!

All the other kids thought the Caldwell family was rich but we were struggling just like everyone else. There were a lot of people in our household.

My father loved flowers and he had them all over the yard: front, both sides, and in the backyard. My mother had a space in the backyard where she planted her garden: beans, collard greens, peppers, etc. Daddy planted flowers and Mama planted food.

We had a mango tree on the side of the house, guava trees in the backyard, an orange tree, a fig tree, a lemon tree, a mulberry tree, and two very large grapefruit trees.

My father also had hunting dogs. It was my job to feed them and keep the "do-do" cleaned up and shoveled into a hole.

I loved to go hunting with my father in the woods at night to get 'coons and 'possums.

Daddy also had traps set in the woods and we had to go out and get whatever was caught in them, and reset them. We lived off the fat of the land. Daddy said that if it got caught in his trap, we were going to eat it. He was quite a good cook too!

I remember one Sunday after Sunday school Daddy said, "Come on boy, we going to pick up a dog." We went out to a town called Midway, about six miles from Sanford. Daddy paid a man $50.00 for a hunting dog named Bell. She was the best 'coon dog I have ever seen.

If a 'coon was out there Bell would find it, and run it up a tree. Then Daddy would shoot it out of the tree. What a team they were! Daddy said, "Boy you better not ever tell your mother how much I paid for this dog!" And I never did! That dog put a lot of food on the Caldwell table.

The big difference between me and my father was that he always said, "I am the captain of this ship, and if it gets to the point where I can't be the captain, I will chop a hole in the bottom of it and sink it!"

My view on this issue is, "I am the captain of this ship, and if it gets to the point where I can't be the captain you can let me off at the next port, and you can sail on!"

This was in reference to being the "MAN" of the house. That is the way he was! The entire household knew it, and the neighbors did too!

My Mother – Catherine (Nelson) Caldwell

My mother was born in the small town of Quincy, West Florida in 1911. Havana and Quincy are near Tallahassee, Florida. Her nickname was *"Mints."* I do not know why. I know she was sweet, easy going, kindhearted, and my relatives tell me I am like her but I look like my father.

My mother is also in the direct bloodline of Native Americans. Her father was a Seminole Indian. He lived in Tampa, Florida.

Much of the research done today indicates that many African Americans who say they are descendants of Native Americans are not truly descendants. Most times people go by family stories, and this is what we mostly rely on. There has been a lot of great work done by Blacks in America but we have done a poor job of recording it for history.

My mother rarely worked (outside of the house) that I can remember. The old men of my hometown tell me that my father was jealous and kept her locked up in the house.

I remember my mother washing and ironing clothes for White people, and I remember on occasion her working in the celery fields of Central Florida. I remember her going to church all the time because she took me with her. She was not going to leave her baby home with those sisters and brothers of mine, no way!

My mother died in February of 1959. I was 13 years old.

I remember my mother whipping me only one time, and that was because I was getting into the chemicals under the sink in the kitchen. She left that kind of thing to Daddy. I think he enjoyed it!

There were times when Daddy was passing out discipline around the house, and you could hear him laughing. Daddy had a tool for whipping he called Caldonia. He would be whipping you with that thing and he would be saying, "Caldonia! Caldonia! What make their head so hard?" Caldonia was made from leather, and it had holes in it with a wooden handle.

I do remember one day Mama must have had a hard time with me because when Daddy came home from work she said, "Denver I couldn't do nothing with this boy today!" I remember thinking to myself, "Mama what the Hell you tell this crazy man that for?" You know the rest of that story: another one of those *"Orange Grove Central Florida Ass Whippings"*!

There were times when I went into the kitchen, looked in the cabinets, looked in the ice box (we did not call it a refrigerator), and I saw nothing to eat.

Mama would go into the kitchen humming an old spiritual song and before long we had a meal. God bless my mother!

My mother used to order baby chickens from Randy's Record Mart in Nashville, Tennessee. They were advertised on the radio station. Some of you may remember the 2 transitor radios. We could only listen to them late at night.

She would order 72 of those little birds. We had chicken coops in the barn in our backyard. I would help her count the birds when they arrived. I would help her take care of them and gather the eggs when they started to lay.

When they were adults and had laid their way out it would be time to kill them for food. Daddy and I would cut off their heads. Mama, and some of the other ladies in the neighborhood, would have the hot water ready and the chickens would be cleaned and stored for food. Everybody in the neighborhood would have fresh chicken for a few weeks.

As I have stated before: in Central Florida we all lived off the fat of the land.

My mother taught me to never tell anyone what you were afraid of because it gave them power over you. She also taught me to never scare anyone (if you knew what they were afraid of) because they could hurt you real bad. I learned this lesson the hard way because I did it to her.

My mother was afraid of frogs and I thought it would be fun to scare her. I was about eight years old and I found a frog in the back yard. Mama was is the house sewing on one of those old sewing machines that you had to pump up and down with your feet.

I came in the house to show her the frog I had found. She screamed out one of those cries that would make your skin crawl, and slapped me down! I slid across the room and, to this day, I don't know what happened to that frog!

I don't remember her taking it out of the house; I don't remember me taking it out of the house, but I never saw that frog again! I never scared anyone with something they were afraid of again!

My mother was a member of what was called a Sanctified Church: "The Church of God and Christ," in Sanford, Florida. On Thursday evenings the congregation would have prayer meeting at 7:00 pm and afterwards they would wash each other's feet.

I thought that that was the worst thing in the world: to have to wash somebody's dirty feet. I am sure many of the members would wash their feet before they came to church, and I am also sure many of them did not.

I can remember times when Mama and Daddy would have their disagreements and the conversations would go on and on. I would just sit, look, and listen to see who would win.

My Daddy was quite a talker you know, and he would just keep fussing. When Mama got tired of it she would say, "Denver, it takes two to argue," and with that said she was through. I knew when she said that she was through. But my Daddy didn't get the message and he would go on and on, all by himself.

Soon he would realize he was talking all by himself, and he would then shut up. I would say to myself, "Daddy, Mama was finished a half an hour ago. I was waiting to see when you would get it. Mama won!"

Daddy used to say," All right *"Mints"* don't make me come over there!" Mama would reply, "Come on over Denver! I got your fare back!" God bless my Mama! That's the way they played.

I remember one time Mama and Daddy were fussing about something and they were getting loud. My sister Verdene ran next door where my mother's sister lived and told her Daddy was going to hit Mama. Of course he was not (that never happened to my knowledge) but Verdene was sure it was going to happen that day.

Aunt Liza came running over to the house and started yelling at Daddy saying, "You better not hit my sister!" Daddy started laughing and said to Aunt Liza, "If I do, what are you going to do about it?" Then Daddy tapped Mama lightly on the arm and said, "There, I hit her. Now do something about it Liza!"

Then Mama started laughing. Then Daddy started laughing. Aunt Liza started laughing and soon the whole house was laughing. Some of us were rolling on the floor with laughter.

My mother teased her sister for a long time about that day! We used to say, "Go get him Aunt Liza!"

My Brother – Rev. Franklin D. Caldwell

My big brother Frank is 12 years older than me. I don't remember a lot about him around the house. He went into the Air Force at the age of 17 which would have made me about 5 years old when he left.

My memories of him are when he came home to visit when he was on leave. I always enjoyed being around him because he was my Big Bro, and then he was gone again.

I really got to know him after I became an adult. I would visit him where he lived in Hampton, and Newport News, Virginia, or he would visit me where I lived in Rochester NY. He was in the Air Force for twenty plus years.

My oldest brother is a man I love but really don't know that well.

As I stated before I remember him coming home on leave from the Air Force: when Mama died he was there; when Daddy died he was there; when we visited each other as adults.

We look alike because when I look in the mirror I see him. When I listen to myself on a recording I hear him; when I laugh I hear him laughing. He is certainly more like Mama than he is like Daddy, but we both look like our father.

When Mama died I remember him saying that the men must be strong for the women in the family. I remember him holding my sisters up at the funeral. I was only 13 years old when Mama died. There were three boys and five girls.

I remember when Daddy died Frank got to all of Daddy's Masonic materials before I got to them.

Daddy died on a Monday and the funeral was scheduled for the following Monday. My father was a 33rd degree Mason. Frank is a Mason, my brother Horrest was a Mason, and I am a 32nd degree Mason. Daddy had a lot of Masonic pins, books, aprons, and other materials.

The week Daddy died was the week I was to receive my 32nd degree. Frank felt that I should come to Sanford the first part of the week (Monday or Tuesday) that Daddy died.

The meeting where I was to receive my degree was scheduled for that Friday night of the same week Daddy had died.

I chose to stay in Rochester for the meeting and then come to Sanford over the weekend because the funeral was on the following Monday. My big brother disagreed with that decision. I felt that Daddy would have wanted me to get the degree as it would have been several years before I would have had that opportunity again.

Two of my nephews, Frankie and Champ, drove down with me over the weekend, after I became a 32nd degree Mason. When I got to Sanford all of Daddy's Masonic materials had been claimed by my two big brothers. (Oh Well)!

My brother is a Minister and after Daddy died he became the head of the family. He will let you know what his position is in the family at the drop of a hat!

When Aunt Eliza died (my mother's sister) Frank was one of the first to arrive, and he took charge. I had been down to visit Aunt Eliza a few months before her death. I had paid off her charge at the corner store where she shopped ($80.00), and I had bought her a half-gallon of gin, (*"toddy"* for the body" she called it) of which she had consumed about half.

She would keep a small half-pint of gin behind the heater in her home. She was so excited when I walked into her house with that half-gallon.

My big brother the minister had thrown a half bottle of gin in the garbage but I got it out. My friends and I drank that gin, and I don't think my big brother was pleased. (Oh Well)!

I remember one time we were all at the dinner table eating. Daddy always sat at the head of the table. Mama sat next to Daddy, and Frank, being the oldest son, sat at the other end of the table facing Daddy.

Frank and Daddy were having a conversation and they were disagreeing about something. We could all see that it was getting a little heated and we knew something was about to happen. Mama was quiet. Everybody else was quiet too. Frank's and Daddy's voices were going up. You did not do that to Denver C!

All of a sudden Daddy picked up a saucer with the pie still on it and that saucer went flying in Frank's direction. The saucer and pie just missed his head and left a dent in the closet door behind Frank.

That dent was there until the house was taken down many years later. Frank got up and ran out of the house. Daddy said, "Now let's eat…" That is the way he was!

My Brother Horrest (Udell) Caldwell

Horrest (Udell) Caldwell or *"Hot Stuff"* is 10 years older than me, and he is a child my father got outside of the marriage. My mother, being the person she was, allowed *"Hot Stuff"* to be at our house as much as the rest of us. So he was really my big brother too.

There is quite a bit I could tell you about *"Hot Stuff"* because he was always around the house. This man would have all of us laughing all the time because he was so crazy!

I refer to him as Udell because that was his mother's family name. When it suited him to be a Caldwell, he was a Caldwell. When it suited him to be a Udell, he was a Udell. (He died in 2004 in Sanford, Florida.)

For many years he lived in Syracuse, New York, which is about 100 miles from Rochester, New York. As most of my family members migrated to Rochester, New York *"Hot Stuff"* lived and worked in Syracuse. We would visit each other often, long before he moved back to Sanford.

When he would visit the family in Rochester he would prepare a meal, and keep it warm under the hood of his car as he drove from Syracuse to Rochester. It would always be on Saturday and all of the family and friends would gather over at Betty's house on the corner of Herman and Thomas Streets. *"Hot Stuff"* would come, and the food was ready.

He used to love to fish so he would arrive with all of the fish he and his friends had caught that day, and the "Fish Fry" was on, right there at Betty's. Betty would call Verdene, *"Tot," "Cat," "Vel,"* and *"Cynt"* and it was on! And *"Hot Stuff"* would start lying!

He used to tell me if one woman didn't work out, get another one! He said there were too many women in the world to be tied down with one, if she was not working out for you. Then he would start lying about all the women he had; and that if one didn't work out he would get another one!

This man looked more like Daddy than any of the rest of us. And he talked trash all the time!

I remember one day we were all sitting on the front porch of the house in Sanford, and something was said or done by *"Hot Stuff"* and everybody was laughing. All of the children, Mama, and Aunt Liza were *"rolling"* about something *"Hot Stuff"* had said.

My big sister Allene was laughing so hard that she could not stop. Mama and Aunt Liza said her *"tickle bucket"* had turned over. They were very serious and had to pour water on her for her to stop laughing. True story!

I had never heard of anybody's *"tickle bucket"* turning over. Have any of you ever heard of such a thing?

For many years after everyone had moved North, and *"Hot Stuff"* had moved back to Sanford, he lived in the old homestead. He tended the place as long as he was well enough to do so.

I remember *"Hot Stuff"* calling and asking for some money. He would call all of his sisters and brothers asking for money: "Hey baby bro', can you spare $50.00?" He would say, "… send it to this address. I am living with this girl for the time being!" Or "Hey baby bro', I am sending you the money order back so you can change the name. All of my ID says Udell down here! Hurry up baby bro', I am broke!"

My Sister – Allene (Mc Elroye) (Marshall) Caldwell

My sister Allene is 10 years older than me. I will always remember her as the one that took care of herself. I remember her working after school to assist in buying her own school clothes. I remember her assisting my mother in keeping the house clean and cooking for the rest of us.

I remember Allene buying her school clothes while Mama had to make clothes for the rest of my sisters.

I remember Allene being a part of the high school band, and marching in the Christmas parade.

I remember her marching in the Homecoming Parade with the high school band.

Allene also left home after high school and moved to Rochester, New York. She married a man named Henry.

They had two children together and eventually were divorced. She then married Melvin (*"Clyde" or "Smilie"*) Marshall, my brother-in-law, and very good friend. She is my big sister that I could always go to for advice, and assistance in life's issues.

I could always go to my brother-in-law for advice and financial assistance too. He was a great brother-in law, and friend.

"Clyde" worked in construction and they would not work in the dead of winter. So I would schedule my vacation for February so I could travel with him and his friends. These men were in their forties and I was in my early twenties. I loved hanging out with these men because I learned so much about life from them.

Allene moved to Rochester, and eventually all of the rest of the family ended up living in Rochester, New York too. My father was the first. He stayed with Allene until he got his own place. My sisters moved up to Rochester and I did too after graduation from high school. The entire family (or at least most of us) got our start in Rochester through the home of Allene Marshall.

I remember when I would leave Sanford on the "Tramp Truck," working my way through Virginia and into New York. When I had worked one week on the camp to get some money in my pocket, I would call Allene to come and get me off that camp, and into the city of Rochester. Then I would go job hunting. I spent one summer with her before I moved to Rochester to stay.

It was the summer of 1964. I had just arrived in Rochester to spend the summer. The riots of that year had just started the Friday night before, and it was Saturday. I found myself walking into an event that changed Rochester for all time.

The city was under a curfew and everyone was supposed to stay home, but nobody did, and all hell was breaking lose.

People were swept into a *"Mob Mentality."* I was new in town and I went along with everyone else. The grocery stores were looted; the liquor stores were looted; the clothing stores were looted; everybody was looting. We were just caught up!

The riots were a result of a lot of things coming to a head in this town. The whole of Rochester was on fire. People were getting arrested. The police were running after people one minute, and the next minute they were running from people! It was crazy!
That entire weekend was a big blur!

The New York State National Guard arrived in Rochester on Sunday and everybody went home.

We called them the *"ass whispers from another world"* (AWAW)! It was a week before things got back to normal, and during that week people drank and ate all that they had looted.

In the mid-1960s in Rochester you could find a job and start working today; then on your day off you could find a second job and start working right away.

After I had lived in Rochester for a while I felt that I needed some discipline in my life so I went to talk to Allene. She told me that I should look into the Masons (she was a member of the Eastern Stars and she liked it). I joined the Masons looking for something to slow me down because I was doing everything, and everybody, ...and the easy ones I did twice!

Yes Masonry helped me, and it changed my life.

I always refer to Allene (*"Tot"* as we call her), as "Sister Marshall" after her late husband. She refers to me as Brother Caldwell because of our masonic connection. I also say that God gave her to me two times: once through our mother and father, and once through the Masonic Order.

My Sister – Verdene (Gathing) Caldwell

I lose track of the years between me and my siblings. I remember Verdene being around the house much more when I was growing up. I can tell lots of stories about the things that happened around the house that involved Verdene because I was older, and I was part of many more experiences.

Verdene was the only child that was not afraid of Daddy. She was the one that would talk back. She was the only one that would fight Daddy when it came time for whippings.

She was the one that stayed in the streets a lot. Verdene would slip out of the house when we were all supposed to be home.

Once, she saw Daddy someplace he was not supposed to be, and came home and told Mama. She was a rebel!

Verdene was the one that would sneak out of the house at night, and then sneak back in after the bars closed.

One night Verdene went out of the bedroom window and left the ladder leaning against the house so she could get back in when the fun was done. While she was out Daddy discovered the ladder leaning against the house, and decided he would wait for her to come sneaking back in.

Daddy was waiting in the dark room. Mama was waiting in the dark room too, praying and crying for her daughter. Then the moment came and Verdene started her way up the ladder (I am sure half drunk)! Verdene got half way up the ladder and Daddy stuck his head out of the window and started shanking the ladder as if he was going to shake her off.

After he had scared her as much as he thought needed he let go of the ladder and let it fall hard back against the house. Verdene was hanging on for dear life as Daddy walked away, going to his and Mama's bedroom. Daddy was laughing, Mama was crying, and Verdene was cussin' like a sailor as she climbed her drunken ass up that ladder and into her bedroom. I was very young when this happened but as I grew older I heard my other family members talk, and laugh, about that night!

When Verdene became of age she moved out of the family house but stayed in Sanford for a while. From Sanford she moved to Miami, where I visited her for a summer. Then she moved to Mexico for a while, and then, like the rest of us, ended up in Rochester, New York. Verdene died in the late 1990s.

I remember one incident, when I was small, and Verdene was still living at home. I was always scared to fight so my sisters protected me, and sometimes fought my fights for me.

Something had happened in school and one of my classmates told me he was going to beat my butt after school. The school bell rang and I hit that door and ran all the way home!

I don't remember this kid's name but he was in hot pursuit, right behind me! I got home, ran in the front door and out the back door, with that kid right behind me!

Verdene said, "Wait a minute, both of you!" She said Fred, "You are going to let someone run you home, into your house and out of your house too? No hell you aint!" Verdene said if you don't stop running, right now and fight, I am going to kick your ass myself!

Well, now it is on, because Verdene was the one in the family that was always in fights. She even tried to fight Daddy one or two times!

I got the plunger that you unplug the toilet with, and I went to work on my classmate. I did not want to have to deal with Verdene. She was MAD! She had smoke coming out of her ears!

Verdene was also a sister we could all go to for advice...mostly because she thought she knew everything, about everything!

I remember Verdene telling me that Daddy was ripping me off. She said, "Fred you up there on Sanford Ave, selling them snow- cones, out there in that hot sun, all day. You make $50.00, and he gives you five? You must be crazy!"

"Well," I asked, "what am I to do Verdene?" She responded, "You take 10 dollars off the top before you turn in the money!" I took my big sister's advice and started taking 10 dollars off the top!

Daddy would give me between 5 and 7 dollars which was plenty for me to play *"Big shot"* at school. In several weeks I had over a hundred dollars under my mattress.

When I saw all that money I started thinking what Daddy would do if he found out I had over a hundred dollars. How would I explain that, and how was I to get rid of all this money? Remember, I am about 13 or 14 years old!

I went to my big sister for advice and she said, "You spend it just like you took it, a little at a time so Daddy would not notice." I stopped taking any money off the top!

I never thought that Verdene would ever marry anybody. She did not have the best feelings for men, and how they treated women. While I was in the Army I heard that my sister Verdene was getting married. I talked with some of my Army buddies and they bet me that she would, and I took them up on it to the tune of $300.00 that she would not. That was a lot of money back in the mid 60's.

She got married, I lost three hundred dollars, and she was divorced in one year!

I had five sisters and I watched how they interacted with men. I thought it was terrible the way they treated their men friends. Allene was married and out of the picture. Betty was one of those women who said, "My Daddy told me what to do all my life growing up. If I did not do it I got a whipping! No man gonna' tell me what to do,... ever!" Betty never married!

Verdene was worst of all when it came to dealing with men. She would keep track of every dime she got from her men friends, or every dime they may have gotten from her, ...and she made sure she stayed way out in front!

Those girls would lie to one man, saying they were sick, in order to go out with the other one. I thought it was very unkind. I learned a lot about how women deal with men from watching my sisters.

My Sister – Betty Jean Caldwell

I always remember this sister as my dancing partner because we danced so well together. We won a swing contest in New Smyrna Beach, Florida. one summer. We were quite a dancing pair.

Betty was called lazy because she would get into trouble for not washing the dishes. Betty would hide those dirty dishes (and dirty pots and pans) in the oven. The oven was the first place Mama or Daddy would look when it was Betty's turn to clean the kitchen.

I don't remember the name of the White radio station in Sanford during the late 1950s and early 1960s, but they would play Black music for one hour each day. They called it the "Rhythm Hour," and it went from 5 to 6 pm each day. That was when we would kick some dust up in our backyard dancing.

The rest of the day they played that Country-Western. We called it "Hillbilly" music.

There are many memories of Betty around the house with Mama, Daddy, and all the rest of that full house. Betty is probably the best cook out of all of the girls. They all had their specialty dish. The whole family loved those baked beans Betty used to make. She also made some homemade biscuits that would melt in your mouth.

Betty moved out of the house and lived in Sanford for a while. She also ended up in Rochester. I lived with her for a while when I first moved to Rochester, and after I got out of the Army. Betty died in the mid-1990s, a few years before Verdene.

When I first moved to Rochester, like the rest of my family members, I lived with Allene for a while. Then I moved in with Betty, at 26 Edwards Street. I think all of us were working at Rochester General Hospital at one point. Allene and I retired from RGH. Betty was the party person and we would have a party at someone's house every two weeks when we got paid.

Girls would bring food and the guys would bring booze. The person at whose house the party was held provided the music. Party all the time, party all the time!

There was one summer when Betty had a party on Edwards Street, and we closed off part of the street so the kids could dance in the streets. All the neighbors took out the grills and cooked late into the night. The music was blasting, the smell of food was in the air, and you could hear it two blocks away. It would appear that we loved to have fun and laugh with people we loved.

Betty decided to move from Rochester and relocated to Tallahassee, Florida for several years. I went and spent some time with her there on vacation. While living in Tallahassee she located many of our relatives on Mama and Daddy's side of the family.

From Tallahassee she moved to South Carolina. She was living in South Carolina when she died.

My Sister – Kathy Jean Caldwell

This is the sister I have the most memories of because we were close in birth, and we are very good friends, too! There are things that *"Cat"* (as we call her) and I did in Sanford and Rochester that if I told you I would have to kill you!

When Mama died, Daddy had to start taking care of children, and that was not his area of expertise. Soon, Daddy had moved to Rochester, took his baby girl with him, and left me and *"Cat"* in Sanford to fend for ourselves.

I was fifty years old before I understood why Daddy had to leave that house. He loved Mama so much that he could not live in that house without her. We were concerned for a while that Daddy had left us alone in that house, but after a while, when things started to go well for us, we forgot, and forgave him for leaving. We were glad he was gone!

"Cat" was in charge of the house. I was there, my niece Vel was there, and my nephew Frankie was there. In the old southern culture the oldest child was always in charge. In many families the oldest child sometimes had to fight for their dominance, but it was understood. When they had to fight they were supported by the parents.

"Cat" was babysitting for some White people, working a little job, and going to college. We were renting rooms to a couple of sailors that were stationed at the Naval Base in Midway. We also rented rooms to the baseball players when they were in Sanford for spring training. I was going to high school, cutting grass, selling snow-cones, and working at Winn Dixie cleaning machines in the meat department. Vel and Frankie's job was to go to school and get good grades. Which they both did!

With young people running the house, and not any real adults there, life was a big party. The people in the neighborhood would always ask how we were doing, and how was our Daddy doing up in New York. We were always to say all is well, because it was. That house was rocking all the time and we were in need of nothing. Oh the stories I could tell you!

There were times that "Cat" had to fight for me, and would not allow me to fight for myself. I will go to the ends of the earth for my Kathy Jean. I could write a book about the exploits of Fred and "Cat" in Sanford!

All of "Cat"'s friends who had finished high school, and some who had not quit, and all of my friends that were still in school, spent time at the house.

We lived at 419 East Third Street, in downtown Sanford. All the stores were on First and Second Streets, so we lived right downtown.

When any of our friends from the surrounding towns and villages came into Sanford to shop, they would all stop by the Caldwell house on Third Street, and hang-out. Party all the time, party all the time, it was a party all the time! There was always a party going on at the Caldwell house on Third Street.

There would always be some girls in the kitchen cooking some food to eat. There was always something to drink. The music was always being played, but not too loud, because we had neighbors who were in contact with Daddy in New York. We all had to play it straight! Everyone who came to the house knew the rules.

"Cat" was working and going to school. I was working and going to school. *"Cat"* had friends that worked, I had friends that worked, and we had the rooms we rented to the sailors, and sometimes to the professional baseball players. The sailors brought some of their friends from the base and the baseball players brought team members to some of the parties. There was always plenty of money.

There were the town *"boosters"* (thieves) who stopped by all the time to rest before they went home. We had plenty of new clothes to wear and there was always food for everybody.

We fed the police when they stopped by. Daddy knew the chief of police when he was living in Sanford, and I would not be surprised if they kept in some kind of contact. That is the way my Daddy worked. That house was party all the time, everyday!

I was living in Rochester and *"Cat"* was still in Sanford. Later on *"Cat"* moved to Rochester too while I was away in the Army. When I returned home I lived with her for sometime, in her home. We have always been close, and good friends.

My Sister – Cynthia Lynette Caldwell

This is my baby sister and they tell me that Cynthia, Fred, and *'Cat"* could pass as triplets, because we look so much alike. The thing that I remember most about Cynthia is she was such a baby, and she let everyone know it!

As an adult she has always been independent, kind of off to herself, and did such a great job of raising her children. She never married but has done very well for herself. We are all very proud of her accomplishments.

Daddy did not leave her in Sanford very long after Mama died. Cynthia finished school in Rochester. Daddy was not able to stay in the house after Mama died and he soon moved to Rochester. Cynthia stayed with us in Sanford for a very short time, then, Daddy got her to Rochester. Daddy left the rest of us there to fend for ourselves and fend we did! One could say he trained us well.

Cynthia had asthma very bad when she was little, and when she would have an attack someone rubbing her belly was soothing for some reason. Mama would always ask me to rub her belly, and she would stick her tongue out at me as I rubbed her belly. That used to make me so mad at my baby sister!

I remember when we were all in Rochester (in Hanover Houses) we would have a family gathering at someone's house each month. We would gather to celebrate the family birthdays for that month.

At one time (I think that Cynthia was still in school or just out of high school) she was having an issue with some girl bullying her. Now Cynthia is the baby of the family and I never knew she had a mean side to her.

In Hanover Houses you could get a *"tailor made" ass whipping"* that wouldn't fit anybody but you! Well, Cynthia had taken as much as she could from this person bullying her, and it was now *"show time."*

Each of the apartment buildings in Hanover Houses had a long fence that went all the way around the entire building. Cynthia and this bully had the entire fence around Building 20 rocking! It was on!

I was at work but they tell me Cynthia did okay for herself, and afterwards she did not get bullied anymore. Now she had a reputation in the projects: *"Cynthia will fight in a minute...or it might take her two!"*

Of course these are all memories now. Oh how we change over the years!

My baby sister has her own home now and is nearing retirement. She has done very well for herself.

My Niece - Velverly Caldwell

"Vel" is my niece, and the daughter of Verdene. Verdene had her very young and my mother took her into our home, and she was always there. Vel is like one of my sisters. We were always very close as children but grew apart as we became adults. My sister *"Cat"* became her mother when our mother died. *"Vel"* also moved to Rochester along with the rest of us.

I remember when Verdene was living in Miami, Florida. *"Vel,"* one of her friends, and I went to spend the summer with Verdene.

We took the bus (Greyhound) and had an adventurous summer in Miami.

Verdene was living in Liberty City and we had sardines and grits for the first time in our young lives. It wasn't that bad! Have you ever heard of such a thing?

Verdene would put us on the bus and give us tours of the different parts of the city.

For some reason Verdene's other daughter settled in Miami and we have a host of relatives living there.

"Vel" was very young when we were all living in Sanford after Daddy left. This may be why I don't have a lot of memories of her while we were growing up.

My Nephew – Frankie Caldwell

Frankie is my nephew, and the son of my big brother Frank. Frank fathered him when he was very young and Mama took him into the house also. Frankie is like a brother and we were raised together. We shared everything, and *"Cat"* became his mother when Mama died.

Frankie moved to Rochester for a while, and then moved to Atlanta, Georgia.

I remember Mama teaching me to share: by sharing everything I had with that damned Frankie! "He was my brother now," Mama would say, "You have to help me take care of him!"

I think even now I still feel that *"evil spirit"* when it is time to share! I have prayed it under control. I thank God for that development (learning to share and give). I thank Frankie and my mother also for helping me to learn that lesson!

I remember Frankie taking me out to Midway (Florida) to hunt rabbits. The rain had flooded the woods behind Midway and we caught twenty or thirty of them. We sold some of them and took the rest home for *"Cat"* to cook. *YEAH!* All of the kids in the neighborhood had rabbit stew, or rabbit *"perlo"* (pileau).

I had to share my clothes, my food, my bed, and my work with Frankie! Daddy made sure everybody shared in the work at home. Frankie would be right there when we were hunting 'coons and 'possums in the woods. He was truly a part of the family. I love him like a brother because that's what he is: my brother!

These are the people that have helped to shape my life. It is said that we are a product of our environment. The people I have been writing about were all a part of my environment (and my life) up to this point.

I love them all very dearly, and I pray for the best for all of them.

I hope getting to know them a little will help you to get to know me better as you continue to read *"One Man's Story."*

Chapter Two

Hometown Experiences

Hopper Elementary School

My family and I lived in a 13 room house at 419 East 3rd Street, Sanford, Florida.

First Street was downtown (where all the stores were) and people came into town to shop, pay bills, and take care of other business.

All of our friends would stop by our house when they were in town so we always had company. Mama was always cooking and we had some great neighbors. Everybody knew everybody! When I was growing up the population (in Sanford) was approximately 11,000 thousand people, and about a third of that was Black people.

We had a long driveway that ran from the front right of our house, down the side of the house, into the large backyard, and then into the garage. My Daddy had all kinds of stuff in the backyard and the garage. He kept everything!

Mama had a large garden in the backyard, and Daddy had flowers planted everywhere. The flowers were planted in the front yard, on both sides of the house, and he had flowers planted in the backyard also.

Once, as an adult (when I had went home to visit), I noticed that the place did not look as large as it did when I was a child. But everything else looked the same!

The old homestead is now gone. My big brother tried to hold on to it as long as he could.

I know how hard it must have been for him living in Virginia and trying to pay taxes on a property in Florida.

I started elementary school at six years of age because many Black children in those days did not go to kindergarten. Many of us did not know what that was.

If you were to visit Sanford today the school I attended has been rebuilt in another location. At the time I attended Hopper Elementary School it was on the corner of Cypress Avenue and 11th Street.

When I was in elementary school if the teacher was called away for some reason she would put me in front of the class to entertain them until she returned.

I would always have some story to tell. I have always been able to take a situation and turn it into a story of some kind. I have always loved telling stories. I got that from my father because he was quite the storyteller.

I lived at 419 East 3rd Street, two houses from the corner of Cypress Ave. We walked to school from 3rd Street to 11th Street, which was a little less than a mile. All along the way to school we would meet friends from adjoining streets and it was a party until we got to school.

The people who lived along the way knew all of our names, knew all of our parents, and cared that we all got to school safely. Doctors lived in the neighborhood. Preachers lived in the neighborhood and our teachers lived in the neighborhood too.

When we got to school the teachers were Black, the cooks were Black, the janitor was Black, and all of the students were Black.

All of the teachers knew all of the parents by their first names, and we could not get away with anything! At that time there was a lot of community love, and every one of the adults was very concerned about our welfare.

Hopper Elementary School went from 1st to 6th grade. After graduating from Hopper we would attend Crooms High. Many of the other schools in the area went from 1st to 7th grade, and then their students came to Crooms. Students came from all parts of Seminole County: Georgetown, Lake Monroe, Altamont Springs, Midway, Goldsboro, Roseland Park, and Oviedo.

The teachers and school officials at Crooms High wanted all of us to do well in school, and make something of ourselves.

I feel one of the biggest mistakes we made as Black people was fighting to integrate schools. If we had fought as hard for separate but equal schools, and won, Black students would be much the better for it.

When the schools in Seminole County were integrated Black teachers lost their jobs, Black principals became teachers again, and White teachers kept teaching what they had been teaching all along, only now with Black students in the room.

The Whites taught that White people had done everything, and Black people had done nothing, ...but cause the Civil War. Many White people are still upset about the Civil War because America lost millions of lives fighting that war. Many of them still feel the Civil War was about slavery. In reality the Civil War was about money, and about holding the nation together. The freeing of the slaves was a by-product of that war.

I remember many of the teachers from those years, and all of the students, because we grew up together. Many of the people from Sanford moved to Rochester trying to get away from farm work. Farm work was all Sanford had to offer a Black person.

I would venture to say that 20% of the African American population in Rochester today has connections to Sanford.

I was in my first year (7th grade) at Crooms High when my mother died. My family's world changed in ways I did not realize until I was well into adulthood.

We were a large and close family. The children left home as they became adults. I wish my family today was as close as we were back then. As we all became adults (and had children of our own) we failed to pass on to our children what our parents had instilled in us. Oh what a shame! As a result of not passing on what our parents instilled in us our family is not as close in the 21st Century as we should be.

There are family members right here in Rochester who do not know one another. The last names may have changed but the blood is the same.

I know I have relatives right here in Rochester now that I would not recognize if they walked up to my the door today! Rochester is not that large of a city that you should not know your relatives, but that is the case.

I believe it is the responsibility of the parents to make sure their children know their grandparents, if they are still alive. It is a wonderful thing for a child to get to know their grandparents. One of the best ways for children to get to know their parents is by getting to know their grandparents.

I remember Mama taking us to Tampa, Florida to visit her father. I remember Daddy taking us to Havana, Florida to meet our grandmother. Daddy would tell us, "There are some ugly people back in these woods but you better not laugh at them, because they are your kinfolk!"

My father was a "Go-Getter" and was always working to keep food on the table. He was gone a lot so Mama ran the home, and raised the children. I don't ever remember wanting too bad for the basic needs of life.

When Mama died Daddy tried to run the house, and finish raising the children. He did-not know how. Daddy also had a hard time living in that house without Mama, his *"Mints."* I can only remember seeing my father cry one time: that was when Mama died.

Daddy was working in the garage and I heard him crying. I was afraid to approach him for I had never seen, or heard, that before. I don't ever remember seeing it again.

Daddy would always be out working in the garage. The garage was his play house. Daddy use to pick up old, broken furniture, fix it up, paint it, and then we would have beautiful yard chairs and tables. We were always having people over for some kind of event. My father was very active in the community.

That may be the reason that when he left us in Sanford (for Rochester) we had people over all the time!

We once had a picture of Daddy, taken in 1939, with other prominent Blacks in our community, at a NAACP meeting. Daddy only had a third grade education.

Mama attended school up to the seventh grade, and she told us that she taught the younger children back in her hometown of Quincy, Florida.

Daddy left *"Cat"* in charge of the house and children and he moved to Rochester, New York, near his now adult children.

"*Cat*" was the "Boss." I was going to school which I loved! My baby sister Cynthia was in Sanford with us for a while. Then Daddy took her to Rochester to be with him. My neice "*Vel*" and my nephew Frankie were with us in Sanford. That left "*Cat*," Fred, "*Vel*," and Frankie to swim or drown. We got us a yacht!

Crooms High School

When I graduated from 6th grade at Hopper Elementary I started going to Crooms High School. Crooms went from 6th grade to 12th grade. I had to ride the bus to school for the first time, and it was a lot of fun!

My mother died when I was in the 7th grade and everything around the house changed. Daddy was home more then, and he became more involved with the childrearing. "*Cat*" was the oldest sibling at home and much of the responsibilities of "running" the house became hers.

I was never interested in making great grades in school so I became an average C student. All I wanted to do was pass, and a C was passing. I regret that now but that was the way I felt. When I speak to children today I tell them if the school gives A's then that is what they should strive for.

My favorite subjects were History, Civics, and Health Education. The only A I received in high school was in Biology because it was such a fun subject.

I tried going out for the football team but the coach told me I was too uncoordinated. I never missed days from high school because I loved going. I made friends easily and I was never in any real trouble.

There was one time when I spent 13 days in the County jail in Sanford. We were riding around in my best friend's station wagon and we picked up some girls. We had some fun, went to the drive-in, and took the girls home.

The next thing I knew I was being arrested and taken to jail for keeping an underage girl out all night. Hell I was underage too!

It took the Sanford police two weeks to get to the bottom of that mess. What they finally found out was that after we dropped the girls off they went out again with some other people and were out all night. Rather than tell their parents they had been out all night with adults they told them they were out with us.

I never told any of the other guys' names and they were never involved. I think that is why I was in jail so long, because I did not tell any names. When the truth was discovered, after 13 days, they let me go.

I will also always believe that Coach Franklin and the Chief of police knowing my Daddy helped out a lot. That is about it…at least that is all I am going tell!

After my short stay in jail the English teacher, Mrs. E. O. Anderson, started teasing me about the incident. She would say in class, "Caldwell, what kind of bird can't fly?" Everybody in the class would laugh. Then she would say, "A jail bird!"

It is funny now, but it was not funny then. I thought my whole life had been destroyed. I had never been close to a jail before. At that point I had never even visited anyone in a jailhouse!

I took French in High school because that class was full of the pretty girls. I took Home Economics in High school because that class had mostly girls in it. I did well in Health classes because I liked the subject, and I loved the teacher, Mr. C.B. Franklin.

Mr. Franklin was the basketball and football coach for the first few years I was in high school. He was a Police officer during the summer months and I would give him free snow-cones all summer long. His beat was Sanford Avenue because that was where the Black folks spent their Saturdays.

In those days if you were a Police officer in the South you could only police Black folks!

Coach Franklin made learning fun, and that made it easy.

Once, when I went home to visit, I heard that Coach Franklin was the bondsman for Seminole County. His office was on French Avenue so we went there. You could see the years on him but he was still Coach Franklin.

I asked him if he remembered me and he started "talking trash" about some of his memories of me in High school. Yes, he remembered me!

I shared with him what a positive effect he had had on my life. I told him that I remembered many of the life lessons he had taught us. He smiled, and thanked me.

A few years ago someone told me that the Coach had died. I was sad because he was one of the few teachers I truly held in high esteem. I am so happy that I had the opportunity to thank him for his example before he passed on!

Crooms High was about 5 miles from where I lived and sometimes we would walk to school because it was so much fun.

I did okay in school because I was always there. I was never in any real trouble, so I learned things from just being in the classroom.

Many of my fellow students were people I had known since 1st grade. My best friend (Eugene A.) and I were raised in the same neighborhood, our parents were friends, and we have remained best friends to this day, even though we are two thousand miles apart.

I started smoking cigarettes when I was in high school. The boys would go to the bathroom between classes and light one up. There would be five guys smoking one cigarette and the fire on the end of that thing would be an inch long.

The bathroom would be full of smoke, like a fire was in there. If a teacher came in the bathroom while there was still smoke in the air, it would be on! If Coach Franklin caught us smoking he would bring out the drum stick and get some butt. God forgive us. We did not know what we were doing! We were not aware that we were developing a bad habit that could last a lifetime.

We thought it was cool to have a pack of cigarettes stuck in our socks, and after school everyone would be bumming one for the road. All I can say to young people is: Never start! Smoking is a hard habit to break.

In High school we had a group we called the *"In-Crowd."* The group consisted of: me, Gene, Sweet Pea, Lawrence Sims, Squire Wright, and a few others. We had only one girl in the group (Audra Hayes) and we would always have a great time studying after school, and working on school projects.

Gene had an old station wagon and we would fill that car up with kids and go to the drive-in theater. We would cover the other kids in the car with a blanket, and Gene and I would pay. Everyone else got in for free.

One night we were going through the gate, the other kids were hiding under the blanket, and Audra started laughing about something. We almost got caught! We had a great time in High school.

I had to repeat 9th grade because of an English teacher who failed me because I hung out with the wrong crowd. Those boys had done some damage to her car because she had given them a bad grade. She just knew I was in on it! But I was not! Really!

As a result I had to spend the summer making up for that class. Then guess who I got for English the next year? The first day of class she told me I would never pass her class. Since my father had to pay for that summer school class, and he would never tolerate me not being able to help him work during next summer, I thought he should know what she had said.

My father said no teacher would say, or do, such a thing. He did not believe me and he refused to have me transferred out of her class. She did exactly what she had promised and I had to go back to summer school the next year. Daddy made me pay for the class the second time, and all that made me graduate one year late from high school.

After the English teacher assured me that I would never pass her class no matter what, I thought, "Why should I go to that class and waste my time?" So instead of going to her class I went to Study hall where my girlfriend had her hour for study.

All through the years of High school I worked jobs after school. I was cutting grass for people, trimming hedges, or cleaning windows. My father kept me very busy. After my father moved to Rochester I kept working because I liked the money, and it helped us survive.

I must admit we had some great teachers who cared if we were successful or not. I went to an all-Black school. The teachers were Black, the janitor was Black, the cooks were all Black, and all of the students were Black. That kind of environment promoted a feeling of ownership. We felt like we owned the place, and the teachers did too.

I was close to graduating from high school when the integration process began. They sent our best students to the White school for the transition period. By the time the process was completed I had been living in Rochester for several years.

I know that I would not have done well in an integrated school because I had gone through too much Black/White stuff in Sanford.

There were a lot of good teachers who lost their jobs as a result of integration. The White teachers taught the same things they had been teaching before: White people did everything and Black people had done nothing but cause the Civil War.

The only kind of work in Sanford at that time was farm work. I knew I was not going to spend the rest my life doing farm work. My sister was doing well in Rochester and, at that time, factory work was plentiful.

On June 7[th,] 1965 I graduated from high school in Sanford. On July 20[th,] 1965 I was working at Rochester General Hospital in Rochester, New York.

Further Education

When I moved to Rochester in 1965 all I had (as far as formal education) was my high school diploma. Soon after arriving in Rochester I was hired at Rochester General Hospital to work in the animal research laboratory. I was taught how to care for the animals and to perform some of the lab tests that were done there. I enjoyed learning these kind of things.

My supervisor was Lee Spidel. He seemed to like the way I worked. My first few months of working I was never late, and he could depend on me to get my work done without having to check up on me.

Mr. Spidel raised quarter horses and he spent a lot of time on his farm in Lima, New York. He said having someone around he could depend on was a great addition to the team.

Then Mr. Spidel informed me that RGH Westside Division would be closing soon and everybody would be moving over to the Northside Division. He wanted me to be the man in charge of the lab but, for that position, I needed some further education. School was the last thing I wanted to hear. He arranged for me to attend courses at the University of Rochester in Animal Science and Animal Husbandry.

Taking care of animals was something I was familiar with because I took care of Daddy's hunting dogs, and I helped Mama with her chickens.

These courses were held at the U of R campus two evenings per week. It was like going to school again, but I enjoyed it because we were studying a subject I wanted to learn about.

This earned me my first Associate Degree.

I did very well in my classes and Lee suggested I continue my education. I liked the subject matter so I said Okay!

I was frequently traveling to conferences in this field, and my love for the subject grew.

Mr. Spidel arranged for RGH to send me to SUNY Delhi for further education in Animal Science. I attended several two week sessions (on campus), and I completed quite a few correspondence courses.

After some time I earned my second Associate Degree in Research Veterinary Technology.

This earned me my second Associate Degree.

By this time I was slowly seeking more opportunities to learn. When I was in high school, and had had some trouble with reading, my father helped me by having me read the Bible every evening. He felt that this was the best book to spend time reading. From that experience I became very interested in the Bible.

I also had by now some experience with correspondence schooling. This was very popular in the late 60s and 70s. This was before the advent of computers.

I enrolled in the Nashville School for Bible Study, and after 18 months I received another Associate Degree in Bible Study from the Nashville Bible Institute.

The Bible Study correspondence course was set up this way: you sent in an application and the fees and the school would send you the books. You would then read the books, and watch lectures on what was then television channel 21. After this the student would take an open book exam, send in the test, and then the school would send you a grade. Now I am seeing As for the first time!

I think my father loved the Bible so much because he used to quiz his uncle Nathan on the Bible. My grand uncle Nathan was said to have memorized the entire Bible. Daddy said he would open the Bible anywhere and start reading a few verses, and uncle Nathan would take it from there! That's what my Daddy said, and I believe him!

I had been trained how to study the Bible from when I was a small boy. Daddy assisted me in reading and studying the Bible in an attempt to improve my reading skills. My Daddy had a third grade education.

I spent every Sunday morning in church with some great teachers who cared if you got it. I read through the entire Bible several times during my 32 years working in the animal lab at RGH. This Bible study correspondence course was an easy one.

This earned me another Associate Degree.

The health field was becoming more and more my chosen field. With my GI Bill benefits I enrolled in Monroe Community College for Nursing. During those years if a man was going to school for nursing he was viewed as *"Homo"*!

There were three men enrolled in the class of 35 students. The other two men were homosexuals but they were extremely helpful in the study group sessions, and great friends. We had a great time!

This was not the case with me but I enjoyed going to school with all these girls (it was like when I was in high school). The study groups were great because after the study session was done the party started! Again, memories from the past!

In order to get your Nursing degree you had to learn the answers to 1500 questions. The State Boards exam had 500 questions, but you never knew which of the 1500 would be on your test.

You had to know the answers to all of them. That required a lot of study group sessions.

This Nursing degree was very helpful in the field of animal research and developmental surgery. When I realized that I was not going to be a nurse, I used the nursing training in animal research. It was extremely beneficial.

At that time Monroe Community College had one of the best nursing programs in New York State.

All of the schooling I have been writing about took place while I was working (sometimes two jobs) and building a marriage with children.

This earned me another Associate Degree.

I was having fun taking correspondence courses and not having to physically go to school, if you know what I mean?

By this time I was feeling that correspondence classes were the way to go. This was of course before the advent of the computers. All I knew about computers (at that time) was that they used zeros and ones, and they were the size of a classroom!

I eventually enrolled (via correspondence) in a Dallas Community College course called "The Earth Revealed" as I had become interested in archaeology. This turned out to be very interesting stuff. Over a two year period of time I earned another Associate degree in Archaeology.

This earned me another Associate Degree.

I was beginning to understand the value of correspondence schooling, and realized that through it (correspondence school) I could continue my education, and work at the same time.

I enrolled in a class at Michigan State University. The school explained that I could get a Bachelor's degree in Phycology in five years through correspondence if I choose. I did! I started in 1983, and completed the degree in 1988. It was a long and hard journey but I completed the schooling and earned my degree.

At the same time I was pursuing my Bachelor's degree I was assisting in the teaching of doctors and nurses in the research lab in surgical technique. I was also providing in-services at the RGH for staff in Cultural Diversity, Sexual Harassment, and Team Building. Teaching adults became my passion.

I was also providing adult training for Action for a Better Community with the ABC Prison Workforce.

These courses started as I advanced in animal husbandry and veterinary studies through Michigan State. Then another door opened for further study. I was in the groove with correspondence study, so we went for it!

This earned me a Bachelor's Degree in Phycology & Adult Education.

In many ways the best education I received was through the volunteer process at ABC. I feel I studied under some of the best minds in that field over a 25 year period of time. While volunteering with ABC I attended numerous workshops on community building and development. I was blessed to travel across the country with masters of this arena.

As I grew to love the Rochester community, its people, and the organizations dedicated to the development of those people, I fell in love with the things I had learned. This education gave me the opportunity to help Action for a Better Community, Inc. take actions to make life for poor people better. This was by far the best education I could have ever received.

Access to the resources at ABC also gave me their assistance in the development of one of this community's best Cultural Diversity Educational Programs yet.

Without a doubt the education, the degree, and the community experience helped to make this the best learning I could have ever received.

Neighborhood Fish Fries

In Florida in the 1950s and 60s, everyone lived off the fat of the land. People tended their own gardens; people had all sorts of fruit trees in their yards; the men hunted, and there was always plenty to eat coming from the surrounding woods, rivers, and lakes.

Many people made their living from the rivers and lakes throughout central Florida. There was always plenty to eat, and plenty to share with your friends and neighbors.

Many of the White land owners trapped on their land. In the case of raccoons, the White people would take the furs and give the meat to the Black people. This was good food because we used to hunt 'coons all the time. If you knew how to cook them, 'coon was good eating!

Each year, when I was growing up in Florida, there would be several groups of people going North (tramp trucks) "following the season" (as it was called), to financially support their family.

Several families would "follow the season" and bring as many workers as they could with them to pick produce like potatoes, beans, apples, cherries, and celery.

I came up to New York twice on the tramp trucks. The first time I came I only spent the summer with my sister Allene. The second time I came I was coming to stay.

Sometimes there would be several trucks with people's belongings in boxes and bags. Most of us did not have suitcases or luggage. Sometimes there would be a bus for the people to ride in. Most of the time people just got in the backs of those trucks and off they went to all points North!

My father would host a big fish fry at our house to see the tramp trucks off for the season. Everyone would come to eat, sing, and pray for the families about to get on the road going North to work.

We would not see those people again until October of that year. The fish fries would take place in June, right after the school year ended.

The hunters would share what they had trapped or shot that week; the fishermen would donate their entire catch of that week; the women would clean and cook fish.

There would be large wash pots filled with hot cooking oil, and as fast as the fish and chicken came out of the hot grease someone would have a plate ready. People would be eating in three adjoining back yards. What a great time for the entire community.

The Chief of police (and some of his crew) would stop by. Firemen from the Sanford Fire Department would come by in the city's one fire truck. These were the same firemen and fire truck that would not come down into the Black neighborhood to put out a fire in a Black home, but they would come to get some of that fried fish!

I remember one year my uncle Authur had killed a black bear and they were cleaning it in the garage. They were cutting it up into little pieces, and putting it in that hot grease and everybody wanted to taste that bear.

Sanford was right on the St. John River, so there was always some fishing going on. There were some people who went fishing every day.

As I have mentioned before my father never gave me money, he made me earn it. I had earned enough money to buy a reel and rod (a "104"). It cost me $15.00 because this was a top-of-the-line reel and rod in those days.

One day some of my friends and I went down to the riverfront to fish. We would always follow the old men because they knew where and when the big ones would be biting.

I caught the biggest fish I had ever seen. I was about 13 or 14 years old and that was a big fish to me! I could not wait to get that fish home so that "Cat" could put it in the pan. But, since I had caught such a big fish, I thought my good luck was working so I decided to stay for a while and try and catch another one.

One of the old Black men said, "Boy, you better get home with that fish before one of these White men take it from you...."

Yes the White men were known for taking good catches away from Blacks and there would be nothing done about it. If the Black people protested they would be arrested. That's the way it was in Sanford, Florida in those days.

When one of the Black fishermen had a good day, they had to hide their fish from the White men who passed by checking, or else they would take your fish! "Give me them fish, nigger! Look like we gonna eat good tonight Joe!" one would say to the other.

At the fish fry the children, especially the boys, would hide near where the men would congregate so we could hear them tell "lies" and jokes. My father was one of the best storytellers you have ever heard.

In these kinds of settings the women would all be together talking, and the men would be someplace else telling jokes. All of the boys would be eavesdropping on the men... we could not let them know we were listening.

We had trees in our back yard. The boys who could climb up the trees to the roof of the garage would have a perfect spot to see and hear everything. These were times when we would hear our dads cuss as they told jokes. They never cussed in front of the children, and we would never cuss in front of the adults.

My father would have those fish fries every year for the people going North to work the season. The preacher would pray a long prayer, the members of the church would sing, and everyone would eat their fill.

The women would be talking to each other (and about each other I am sure), and the men would be off someplace secluded telling "men" jokes. Those were the days! The children would be playing games, "ripping and running" all over the place.

There would be plates of food being passed across fences, and someone would take a plate to the old people down the street who were homebound. It was just a great time for friends, family, and community.

Playing Sandlot Football

When I was growing up in Sanford the schools were segregated: all the Black kids went to Crooms High School, and all of the White kids went to Seminole County High School.

The White schools played White schools in sports, and the Black schools played Black schools.

At certain times during the year we would meet the White boys at the city stadium and we would play each other a rough and tumble football game. It would be the Whites against the Blacks. The stadium would be closed on Sundays so we would all climb over the high wall around the stadium, and it would be on!

We were not really there to play football. We were there to hit each other as hard as we could. The score did not matter to either side. What mattered was who hit the hardest, and who drew the most blood. The word would go all around town, to the White school and to the Black school. The adults were not told what we were doing. We did it two or three times each year.

In Central Florida it was football season year in and year out. The weather was always great! Some of the participants would be recent graduates, and sometimes grown men on each side. They had to at least look young in order for us to let them play. It was real warfare!

The most noted Black football players from Crooms High, and the most noted White players from Seminole High were always there. I don't remember anyone ever getting seriously injured but there were always busted lips, black eyes, and sore bodies.

This was the only time we could play with the White kids of the community. It was like the Super Bowl of Sanford Florida.

There were no girls there because we were afraid they would tell someone. It also could have been because everyone had to climb over the wall at the stadium.

Some of the players were recent graduates of both schools, and some were young people of the community who knew we were going to be there, and what we were doing.

There were few fights and everyone knew it was going to be hard hitting football.

This was also how we got to know some of the young White boys in Sanford.

We played four full quarters. Some of us had to umpire the game to make sure it was played as fair as possible.

The one game that comes to my mind is when those White boys beat us 30 to 6. We busted them up pretty good that day! They won the game, but we won the football fight!

We all shook hands, climbed over the wall, and went home.

I have tried to figure this out over the years: Why? In an environment where our parents would have had fits if they knew what we were doing (both Black and White kids); in an environment where Blacks and Whites were really at odds with one another; we children still wanted to engage in the business of being children: "To Play."

Why, in an environment of hatred and misunderstanding, we would lay all that aside to play a game of football? I am sure that after the game was over and we all went back home, the hatred and name calling resumed; it sure did in my house.

My father would have killed me if he knew I was playing football all afternoon with White boys! In his mind he would have been worried about my safety.

There were many times Blacks played with Whites and were never seen again! It was common to hear about some Black person found dead out in the woods.

Martin Luther King Story

I was in high school (Crooms High School, Sanford, Florida), and the Civil Rights Movement was in full swing. I don't remember Dr. King ever coming to Sanford but everyone was aware of the Movement. Everyone!

I remember Civil Rights workers coming to Sanford and recruiting high school students and community people to participate in the marches and the sit-ins that were being planned and scheduled. Several of my friends, and my sister, volunteered to participate. The Civil Rights workers received a lot of help from community residents.

The volunteers had to attend meetings, and rallies, where they were trained how to protect themselves when the police beat them with the clubs and sticks. They were trained how to protect themselves from the dogs the police had for crowd control. They were trained how to conduct themselves at sit-ins when White folks spit on them and poured milk on them as they sat at the *"Whites Only"* counters.

They were trained in the principles of "Non-Violence" and how to react when spat on, beat on, and when the dogs were put on them. My sister came home from this training so enthused about all of the remarkable things they were learning about Dr. King, and this great Movement.

Not all of the members of the Black Community were happy about this Movement. Some were outright opposed to it because the Movement made some White folks very angry.

Things could get real rough for Black folks when White folks were angry about something… anything!

Sanford, Florida was not a happy place when the word got around that "....those Civil Rights workers were in town." There were prominent Black folks on both sides of this issue.

There are those Black folks who say they marched with Dr. King, and that they supported the Civil Rights Movement of the 1960s. Some of them are telling the truth, and some of them are lying too!

Some of those who understand what the Movement means now, in hindsight, did not understand what it meant then. There are many Black people who need to just tell the truth about how they felt then. Just tell the truth, it's okay!

As we celebrate the 50th anniversary of the March on Washington it is good to see all the people who have benefitted from all of the sacrifices that were made by those marchers, and Civil Rights workers. I was pleased to see the first Black president of this country at the celebration. It was a great thing that President Clinton and President Carter were there. But where were President George Bush and his dad?

I am also wishing, and praying, that many of the people who were alive at that time will tell their story as to why they did not support the Movement. I think many did not participate because of fear and misunderstanding.

There were many Black people living in the South that were vehemently opposed to what the Civil Rights workers were trying to do. There were many! But today these same people are claiming they were part of the marching, and sit-ins that took place. They are lying!

I told those Civil Rights workers that I got spat on by White folks passing me by in their cars; I told them that I got called Nigger on an ongoing basis by White folks.

I told them I did not have to join a Civil Rights group for White police officers to beat me with their sticks.

The White police officers beat us with their sticks enough when they would catch us doing some of the crazy stuff we used to do. I asked why do I have to go downtown for all this to happen? I told them that it happened in my neighborhood every day! (I did not see the big picture!)

The only picture I could see was: If White folks spit on me, I am spitting right back on them! I was not going to sit at a drugstore counter downtown and let White folks crack eggs on my head, sprinkle salt and pepper on it, and I just sit there? Hell No! Oh, Hell No!

Daddy said, "Fred, it would be better if you stay home!" So I stayed home! I did not join the marches and I did not participate in any of the sit-ins. At the time I was too young, and I had had too many bad experiences with White folks in Sanford.

I am eternally grateful to Dr. King, and all the people who did what they did during the Civil Rights Movement. I was young, and I did not understand. I was one of those Black folks who said, 'Non-Violence my ass! If we gonna fight, let's fight! If you hit me, I am going to hit you some too! Win or lose!"

There was no way I was going to let the White folks do all the fighting by themselves. I was going to fight some too! That was the reason Daddy told me to stay home.

I remember one day I was riding my bicycle down Sanford Avenue. A truck with some White men in and on the back of it passed me. They threw a bottle of pee on me as they passed, and rode away laughing and yelling: "Take this home with you nigger!" I went home crying and told my mother what had happen.

She started crying too as she took off my clothes, threw them away and cleaned me up. I did not need to join a protest group to get treated badly.

When people in the South have racism in their heart, be they Black or White, that is where that feeling is, and it cannot be easily moved. Racism is usually instilled in people at a very young age. Racism is hammered into a heart and designed to last a lifetime.

So when some White folks heard the Freedom workers were in town the hatred boiled in them. When some Black folks heard the Freedom workers were in town fear reared its ugly head, and they knew things were going to get bad. A Black person may have been ready to get a loan from the bank that they really needed, but now they knew that that loan would never happen!

This was the effect it had on the entire community.

White people did not hate my father any harder than he hated them. My father told me many times that the White man had no good in mind when he was dealing with Blacks. He said, "Son, you need to understand that, and never forget it or you will find yourself in a place from which you cannot escape."

I was forty years old before I could bring that hatred under control. It took me that long to allow everyone to show me who they were without me pre-judging them.

I am a better person now as a result of those life experiences that taught me to treat everybody the same, and allow them to prove who they are through their words and actions.

Now that I am older I find myself regressing. I have come to the conclusion that there really has been very little change! There have been many changes since those days, ...and many things have not changed. It just seems to me that there are just new people doing the same old things!

The Christmas Parade

Each year the city of Sanford and Seminole County would have its annual Christmas Parade. The parade would travel right down Sanford Avenue. There would be floats from all of the schools and other organizations such as the Boy Scouts, Girl Scouts, the Crooms High School band (Black), and the Seminole High School band (White). There would be floats from all of the elementary schools, and there would be a police car with flashing lights that would mark the beginning of the parade.

The Black people would line up on both sides of Sanford Avenue from 7th Street to 2nd Street going towards downtown. There would be no one from 2nd to 1st Streets as that was the line of separation of the races. The parade would then make a left turn onto 1st Street where all the White people would line up on both sides of the street to watch the parade pass by.

As the parade passed down Sanford Ave the Black groups would put on a show. The Crooms High school band would play some Black music that was popular at the time, and the little children would do flips and turns as all of the Black people shouted and cheered.

The White groups would do nothing but walk down the street silent, looking at both sides of the street, and at all the Black people.

Then when the parade turned onto 1st Street the Black groups would go silent, and the White school bands would put on their show. That was the way it was!

70

Based on the way this Zimmerman trial is going, it is still that way!

The next to the last thing in the parade was Sanford's one fire engine with Santa Claus on top, throwing out candy to all of the children. This one fire truck, with eight or ten White firefighters riding on it, would race the engine, and sound the siren.

There were no Black firemen at that time. This was the same firetruck that would not come into the Black neighborhood to put out a fire (down in the "Black quarters" as it was called). They would call it "Nigger" quarters!

Right behind the fire engine walked the Klux Klux Klan in full uniform. No one would say a word when they passed by. Many of us could tell who they were by their shoes and the walk that some of the town's White men had.

The fire chief always wore cowboy boots, and the man who ran the corner store always wore those old red hunting boots.

We would get as much candy as we could, and then go back to playing, hoping for a toy or two for Christmas.

When the Klan walked down 1st Street in front of the White people, we could hear the cheers for them....

I wish we could get the young Black people of today to understand what their parents and grandparents had to endure for them to have the right today to ignore their history.

There is a lot of meaning in this Christmas Parade story about the way things were in the Deep South during those times. Look at the meaning behind the fact that all of the Black people viewed the parade on Sanford Avenue. They were not allowed to view the parade on 1st Street, that was for Whites only.

—

Look at the meaning behind the fact that the all-Black Crooms High School band was at the back of the parade. Black groups were never in front of the White groups. The Black groups were always walking behind the animals and they had to watch out for the horse poop! At this time there were more cows in Florida than in Texas.

The band put on a show for the Black people on Sanford Ave; but they just walked by the White crowds on 1st Street. The Black band was not allowed to perform on 1st Street. All this was part of the game to keep the Blacks in their place.

Look at the Klux Klux Klan at the end of the parade and the meaning behind that. Not a sound was heard when they passed down Sanford Avenue, in front of the Black crowd. But they were cheered on 1st Street by the Whites. Do you get the meaning, and why young Black people say they don't want to hear about those days? Sad! Sad! Sad!

The Neighborhood Giants

There was a couple who lived in my neighborhood and we kids called them the giants. The husband's name was "Slim" Grant, and his wife's name was Celestine Grant.

Mr. Slim was seven feet tall and weighted about 400 lbs. He was a big man. He always wore overalls. That was all he could wear.

Mrs. Celestine was 6 ft. 7 in., and she weighed about 375 lbs. She made all of their clothes because they could not find any at the stores that would fit!

They were wonderful people, and they loved children. All of the children would spend time at their house because Mrs. Celestine would cook those very large biscuits, and what they called hoe-cake bread, and potato pone. She would cook all day, and when Mr. Slim came home, he would eat it all.

During the day she would feed all of the neighborhood children, and tell us stories just to keep us around. I don't know if she knew it but she did not have to tell us great stories, all she had to do was feed us some of that great cooking, and there was always so much of it. Those two people could eat a lot of food.

The story I want to share about Mr. Slim is his not liking cats. One weekend when he had been drinking and on his way home, he saw a cat and several kittens. He picked up one of those kittens and through it a city block. "Let's see if you land on your feet!?" he said.

I feel sorry for that incident today but that was the funniest thing we kids had ever seen. Sanford is a small town but the city blocks were average in length. Mr. Slim tossed that kitten from 5th Street behind the pool room, to 4th Street behind Tip-Top food market.

Another time Mr. Slim had been drinking and a policeman decided that he was going to arrest him. Mr. Slim told the policeman that he would turn himself in after he went home and had gotten something to eat. The policeman would have none of that, and he called for back up.

By the time the other five officers arrived, all of the people had come out of their homes, and a big scene had developed. Mr. Slim went in the house to eat.

All six of the White police officers rushed into the house to make the arrest. Mr. Slim would come to the door and through one officer out, and then Mrs. Celestine would come to the door with another one. Those officers were flying in the air when they came out of that house!

We laughed that day until some of us were crying. Those White policemen were completely embarrassed.

The Chief of police told those young officers that if Slim said he was coming to turn himself in, you can rest assured that that was what he was going to do. The Chief told them that Slim was a man of his word! The Chief had arrested Mr. Slim many times before.

After Mr. Slim had eaten all the food Mrs. Celestine had cooked that day he went downtown and turned himself in to the police. He only had to walk five blocks to the police station he lived right up from downtown. The White man that Mr. Slim worked for had him out within an hour, and Mr. Slim was drinking again. That is what Slim did: worked all week on that White man's farm, and got drunk on the weekends. All the people in the neighborhood loved them so much. They were "Big Fun".

Sometimes Mr. Slim would play in the streets with the children; he would teach us how to shoot pool in the pool room, and he would bring us goodies from the farm where he worked. He and his wife just loved children. They had a very large son late in their lives. He became a very large man too!

There were other very interesting people who lived in our neighborhood.

As a child I remember a man with one arm. They called him "Sanka." I was very afraid of this man because I had never seen anyone with one arm before. My mother told me he lost it in an accident. All I knew was I did not want to get too close to him. I would run every time I saw him!

My friends and family knew I was afraid of him so they would tease me by saying, "Fred here come "Sanka," and I would run home to my Mama crying! When I look back on it I can't find a good reason why I was so scared of that man. He got along well with all of the community members. He was always at the fish fries, and I would always see him around town. My Mama tried to get me to touch that cut off arm,... but not in this life!

There was also a man named James who lived in our neighborhood. He was in his twenties but he was about seven years old mentally. He would play ball with the children in the neighborhood.

He would chase us pretending that he was going to kill us when he caught us. He could not talk very well but he could make some strange noises that scared us so much.

One day James was chasing us and I stepped on a nail in a piece of old wood. I was yelling to the top of my voice, and bleeding all over the place. James picked me up, and took me to my mother who was working in the back yard. He understood that I was hurt, and took me home.

There were some good people in the neighborhood where I was raised. All the adults took good care of the children, and all the parents were good friends.

Today we don't know our neighbors' names, and you better not say anything to their bad-ass children!

I am told that today you need to know your neighbor well enough for them to call 911 on your behalf if needed, and you do the same for them. I believe you need to go further but very few people agree with me!

I thought it was all right!

I grew up in Central Florida during the late 1950s and the early 1960s. These were times when Black people were doing positive things for the advancement of their people, but many things were done undercover. The only people who knew what was going on were the people that it impacted directly.

There are those who say that racism was worst in Texas, Alabama, and Mississippi. Let me tell you that Florida and Georgia were not far behind!

I was so caught up in the style of the times, I never thought I was being discriminated against until I moved to New York State and started college. That was when I found out about all of the things that Black people had done to make this country great.

I had thought it was all right for me to go to the side of the building and buy a nickel hamburger through a small hole, ...while White people went inside to eat.

I thought it was all right for me to drink out of one water fountain, and that White people drank out of another. It just did not matter to me as a child. I was a product of the "Willie Lynch" brainwash. We are all products of our environments.

I thought it was all right for the White kids to get new books, and we were so happy to get the used ones from the White school. They were new to us!

I thought it was all right for the one fire engine in Sanford to never come into the "Black quarters" (where Black people lived) and put out a fire. If a Black home caught on fire, you better get out! Then, when the fire went out, we would help rebuild that family's home.

Some White people would come down into the "quarters" to help rebuild a home after a fire. Some of those who came to help were firemen! I thought it was all right.

Just think how crazy racism is when a community spends twice the money for two sets of bathrooms, two sets of water fountains, etc. Two of everything cost twice the money! Maybe they did not understand either.

I thought it was all right for a young White man to call my Daddy "boy" when we were working for them. My father was old enough to be his father, and they called him boy, …and he answered them, "Yes sir." I thought it was all right. When I would ask my father about these things, he would say, "Things will change, and you won't have to go through this." I believed my father so I thought it was all right!

As a youngster growing up in Sanford, Florida I thought it was all right for the land owner who posted his land to call us "niggers" when we hunted on his land. We knew what posted signs meant! Being called a "nigger" was almost an everyday event. We had grown accustomed to it.

I thought it was all right for the police to arrest a Black man for looking at White women. After all we had been taught all of our lives that White women were off limits to Black men. I was not aware of our history at that time and I was not being taught about the mixture of people that had gone on for centuries.

I thought it was all right for us to celebrate "Negro History Week." Now we have "Black History Month" and we can talk about all the contributions that Black people made to the building of America. But when I was growing up it was one week. There usually was a school play and speeches done by different teachers and students.

Someone would always recite James Weldon Johnson's, "The Creation" while someone else acted it out. Someone would tell the story of George Washington Carver and the many things he did with the peanut. We would always remember Bethune-Cookman College and its founder (a Black female). The school was only 32 miles away in Daytona Beach.

That was it! Those were the only Black people that had ever done anything worthwhile, and we talked about them every year, once a year!

We have to remember through it all, there have always been some good White people. There were good White people who fought slavery from its beginning to its end. If it were not for some good White people, who risked their freedom and their lives, many Black people would have never learned to read. The Underground Railroad would have been a failure if it were not for some good White folks who helped to hide the escaping slaves.

Back then I felt that way because that was what I had been trained to think, and feel. I thought everything was fine. I thought it was all right!

Thank God for Rochester, New York, Rochester General Hospital, Action for a Better Community, and all the great people who have helped me to see the big picture through education.

D. C. the Entrepreneur

I want to tell you about how my father earned money. First you need to know that we never wanted that badly, for anything. There was always something around the house to eat, even if I could not find it. Mama would find it somehow!

We always received a toy or two for Christmas, and a few pieces of new clothing. There were always a lot of mouths around the table to feed, including our neighbors and friends.

At Christmas time Daddy would go out in the yard late at night after we had gone to sleep. He would take a horse shoe and make a set of prints and make marks on the ground. When we woke up on Christmas day he would tell us that the reindeer and Santa's sled made those marks. I believed in Santa Claus until I was about 12 or 13 years old. Verdene would always tell the rest of us that Daddy was not telling the truth.

D. C. would always pray one of those long Baptist prayers before we started eating our large Thanksgiving and Christmas day meals. I still don't remember Daddy working for anyone. The man never worked for anyone else, but always worked. But he always had something to do that would put some money in his pocket or some food on the table.

In the neighborhood we call a person like that a "Hustler." In the suburbs they call a person like that an "Entrepreneur." I don't think he did anything that he would have to go to jail for, but I am sure he came close a few times.

I am almost sure that my father never heard the word entrepreneur, but that is what he was. An entrepreneur is a person who earns money through "ideas not common." These can be things that other people won't or cannot do!

As I shared with you in the introduction to my family at the beginning of this book, I know my father did all kinds of work, because he always took me with him. (I hated when school was in recess, because that meant I had to work alongside my father.) All summer long I had to go to work while the other children played!

Daddy came up with the idea of selling snow-cones and he started the business up and running himself. First he made a box that held the ice and flavor (he mixed the flavor himself). This box was on a frame that sat on two bicycle wheels which he built himself. The box held one 50 pound block of ice. When he saw he could make money this way he built a box that would hold two 50 pound blocks.

The first box he built he pushed and walked behind it. The second one was attached to a bicycle and he rode it all over town.

Once the business was really booming Daddy purchased a motorcycle and built a frame that would hold four 50 pound blocks of ice, flavor, cups, and other supplies he needed for an entire day.

Whenever he ran out of ice or other supplies he would get to a phone, call me and I would take him more. Back then there were no phone booths or cell phones. Daddy had to stop at someone's house that had a phone or at a business that he knew. There were not many people who had phones in their homes in those days.

I think one reason Daddy made sure I could drive was to help him in his business. The man made good money selling snow-cones, and I did too. I used to take the first cart he made up on Sanford Avenue on Saturdays and earn $50.00 in one day. That was a lot of money in those days. We did very well.

Even later Daddy bought a little truck, and then it was on! We would go to Daytona Beach on holidays and we would make $200.00 in one day selling snow-cones. That's the truth! This was in the late 50's and early 60's.

When leaving to sell snow-cones Daddy would put on his white shirt, his white pants, black shoes, and a white apron. When he came home in the evening that white shirt and apron would have all of the colors of the flavors he sold that day. He would have a large bag full of coins, and a roll of dollar bills that would choke a mule.

All of us would gather around the dinner table to help him count the money. One of us would be responsible for counting dimes and another one of us would count the dollars. My job was to count the pennies and then to roll them in paper coin rollers so that Daddy could take the money to the bank.

Daddy told me (after I had become an adult) that he knew we were taking some of that change.

I think Verdene counted the quarters and she always got her a few dollars. Daddy said that that was why he never gave us any money because he knew we were taking some!

I never knew he was aware of what we were doing. I never thought he was the type that would allow such a thing. I guess I did not know the old man as well as I thought.

I remember when Daddy taught me and "Cat" how to make the flavor. The main ingredients were: lots of sugar, lots of water, and the special flavors he used to mail order from somewhere.

Every so often we had to take the ice shavers apart and sharpen the blades so that when you scraped it across the ice it would fill up with finely shaved ice. In Sanford the weather was always hot, and those snow- cones hit the spot! As the ice melted and mixed with that sweet flavor it became better and better to the last drop.

Five, ten, and fifteen cents were the prices we charged, and that change added up fast! We had grape, strawberry, and "tutti frutti" (something Daddy made up) flavors. Everybody loved those snow-cones! I would guess that all together we had ten different flavors, and we made them all.

When my cousin Elbert came to live with us Daddy had him selling snow-cones on the bicycle cart. It was a good business!

I believe a snow-cone business could work today, but you would have to kill these young people because they would try to steal the money you earned on side streets, and main streets too! Times have really changed! The city of Rochester is much too dangerous for that! I hope it is not fear that keeps me from trying, but common sense.

I will tell you one story. My father was a Mason, he belonged to the NAACP, and he was a member of some Black voting community effort. He sold snow-cones to everybody in Sanford, and everybody knew him.

My father had a third grade education but some of his friends were doctors (Black, we had three in Sanford) and Ministers in the community. He was on a first name basis with all the teachers. The Chief of police knew my father, and Daddy did work for some of the most prominent White people in our community.

He had to have a license to sell things, and to hunt certain things. Daddy knew all of the right people in Sanford.

When I was thirteen years old my father told me, "Boy there are two kinds of people in the world: those that buy, and those that sell.

The money always ends up on the side of those people selling. You have to decide which side you want to be on!" That was not a hard decision for me because Daddy always had some money. At an early age I knew the value of money, and what it could do.

Daddy had a hiding place in the garage where he kept a Prince Albert can with a roll of money in it. He and I were the only ones that knew his hiding spot. He told me not to tell anyone, not even Mama. I never did!

Ever since then I have always been selling something. I sold snow-cones in Sanford. I sold Shaklee Vitamins door to door here in Rochester. I sold Amway products here in Rochester, and I had business partners in three states. I bought and paid for a 1979 Chrysler New Yorker (money green was the color) by selling Amway products. I learned Daddy's lesson well.

Daddy managed a rooming house on Thirteenth Street that had an enormous back yard. It was next door to Snow's Restaurant in Goldsborough.

I learned to drive a car in that back yard because we spent so much time over there.

I will never believe that Daddy owned that property by himself, as he tried to make us believe. I believe that Daddy, Dr. Starkes, Dr. Ringling, and some others went into this venture together. I don't put anything pass those men of old. They were very clever, and they knew how to make it.

The men who lived in the boarding house rented rooms, ...and some of those rooms were used for other purposes I am sure. There was one lady who prepared meals for the boarders. Daddy had an office on the first floor, and the kitchen was in the rear of the building.

I remember one day we saw Daddy coming home from managing the rooming house. His clothes were torn, his knuckles were bruised , and his lip was bleeding. I said, "Daddy you look like you were in a fight?" He said," You should see the other fellow!" We had a big laugh that day!

Daddy said if anybody saw that other fellow, they would know he had been in a fight also! Daddy said he had to make a man move out of the rooming house. He had told the boarder, "If you can't pay one week's rent, how do you plan to pay two?"

When Daddy lived in Rochester he operated a store on North Street. He sold all kind of used items and household things. I don't know if he made any money, but he was there. If I know D.C. he was doing all right.

When he moved back to Florida he had us help him load all those old items from his store onto the back of a truck, and he drove back home. Daddy said he could sell an Eskimo an air conditioner, and an African a space heater!

Once, when he was sick and we had to go to Florida and visit him, we found the house was full of old stuff. Some of it was the stuff he had brought with him from New York. I told him he was living in a fire trap. Daddy responded that somebody might need those things.

After he died, we threw all of that stuff away! He was always trying to sell somebody something. I am that way too about selling things, but I don't like holding on to old stuff. That is the way I was trained!

Thanksgiving Dinner / Sanford, Florida

When Daddy left Sanford and moved to Rochester NY, he left *"Cat"* in charge of the house and all of the children. He did not leave his baby daughter in Sanford very long. He soon brought her to Rochester to be with him. *"Cat"* was in charge and Freddie Lee, Frankie, and Vel were there all together.

Many of the townspeople were concerned about our welfare, but there was no need to worry: we were all doing fine.

The townspeople expressed their concerns about our welfare, but I don't remember them ever giving us any money (unless they gave it to *"Cat."*). She never said they gave her any money, but they did plenty of talking about D.C. leaving those children in that big old house alone!

As I have stated before *"Cat"* was going to school in Daytona Beach (college), and she was working small jobs around town. I was also working small jobs around town (cutting grass, selling snow- cones, cleaning the meat area at Winn Dixie on Saturday evenings), and going to school, which I loved.

All *"Vel"* and Frankie had to do was go to school and bring home good grades.

We were some of the best dressed kids in town because all of the *"booster's"* goods came through our house. *"Cat"* got the pick of the best. We were wearing all of the latest fashions. We were the trend setters. All of the thieves stopped by our house to rest before they went home. That is all I am going to say about that!

"Cat" had lots of friends, and I had a lot of friends. All of them could hang at our house as long as they wanted because we were in charge. *"Party all the time! Party all the time!"* Life was a party all of the time!

At our house there was always a houseful of young people playing games, cooking food, drinking booze, and partying all of the time.

We did have study groups at our house when exam time came at school. We were a team and everybody helped out when and where they could. I can't call names because then I would have to kill you! We knew nothing about "hard drugs." We drank a lot! I did not know anything about "pot" until I came to New York.

We used to have house meetings to tell the young people who spent time at the house how to deal with nosy people asking questions about what went on in the house. A lot went on that "nosy people" did not need to know about, and we developed a process of what to say, and who to say it too. We had a system.

We were well aware that Daddy was in contact with some of the adults in Sanford whom he had instructed to keep an eye on things while he was away.

We had a meeting with all of the young people who came to the house and decided we would have a big Thanksgiving Dinner at the house. There had to have been about 75 young people coming to the dinner. There were about 15 core planners. The core planners were the ones that were always at the house, almost every day.

These were the rules:

1. We would have everything you could imagine people had for Thanksgiving Dinner (everything).
2. Everything had to be stolen. Nothing could be paid for with money (nothing).

Each of the team members were responsible for bringing certain items, and everything had to be stolen.

Those girls spent two days cooking and preparing food for the big day. The neighbors had to wonder where in the world those children got all of that food, booze, and music from? It was a party to remember!

We had a cleanup team for the house, a cooking team for the food, and a yard team for setting up tables in the backyard and in the barn. All of the neighbors from down the street were invited and there was plenty for all. The party lasted from the Wednesday before Thanksgiving to Sunday afternoon: we all had to get ready for school on Monday.

And everything had to be stolen! I remember when the booze was stolen and we hid all of that liquor upstairs. What a ball! I remember when one of our large friends walked out of Winn Dixie with a whole turkey between her legs, and we laughed until we cried, all the way home.

There was food and people eating on the front porch; there was food and people eating inside the house; there was food and people eating in the backyard. You could hear the music and laughter three houses away. There were people who happened to be passing by that we didn't know who stopped in and had some food and fun. That Thanksgiving Dinner was quite a time, and I know some people remember!

I don't ever remember any fights among all of those young people, even with all of that booze around. At that time I had never heard of anything called "pot," or marijuana.

I pray that God will forgive all of those young people for what they did. Please forgive us Lord, we did not know what we were doing. But it was fun, and no one got caught!

Parents Supporting Teachers

When I was in high school I did not pass 9th grade English. I had to go to summer school. Daddy was very upset because I could not help him work as much that summer. I was in school and Daddy was cutting grass and cleaning peoples' windows alone.

Daddy was working alone that summer and I was going to summer school, and could not hang out with my friends. That was a bad summer!

When summer was over and it was time to go back to school, I had the same English teacher that had flunked me the year before. You would never get the same teacher in summer school that you had during the regular school year. Summer school was fairly simple: all you really had to do was be there.

The first day of class my English teacher told me, "Freddie Caldwell, you can make 50 As in this class, and you will not pass!"

After the summer Daddy and I had had, I knew he was not going to allow me to stay in this woman's class once I told him what she had said. Remember, Daddy had to pay for that summer class I attended. My having to attend summer school cost Daddy and me money. But Daddy supported the teacher anyway!

He said, "You lying boy! That teacher never said that!" Daddy never questioned the teacher! I had to stay in that woman's class the whole year, and she flunked me a second time!

I had to go to summer school again, but Daddy had moved to Rochester, and I had to pay for summer school.

My mother died when I was in the seventh grade. Daddy stayed in Sanford a few years after Mama's death.

By the time I reached the ninth grade (or about that time) Daddy moved to Rochester. So I had to pay for summer school myself.

I was glad when some of my friends (whom she flunked also) broke out the windshield in her new car! Goodie! I will never tell. That English teacher always believed that I had something to do with the damage done to her car. I really was not part of that. Really!

This story illustrates how the teachers and the parents worked together for the education of Black children in Black schools. Usually the kind of support my father gave to the English teacher worked to the benefit of the student. In this particular case it just went bad. But, Daddy was right to support the teacher; the teacher was wrong not to give me a second chance.

Most parents in a Black community of a small town like Sanford knew each other. A lot of them went to the same churches, belonged to the same clubs, and saw each other all the time. The parents were concerned about the safety and well-being of all of the children in their community.

Many of the same teachers taught all of the siblings in a family. It made sense for the teachers and parents to work together. I am glad that they did work together or my early school years would have been much worse!

The parents in those days even supported the teachers putting the paddle to our butts in school. I remember Mrs. Holly and the palmetto switch. I remember the coaches in high school putting the paddle to our butts.

Depending upon the relationship your parent had with a teacher you may have gotten even more punishment when you got home. Teachers and parents really worked together. Now I see it was all for our betterment.

Going to Sunday School

My mother and father were both active in their churches. For some reason I gravitated towards my father's church: Zion Hope Missionary Baptist Church.

Daddy and I always attended Sunday school. We would stay for morning services which lasted until about 2 pm. We would then go home, and I would return at 6 pm for youth services, Baptist Young Peoples Union (BYPU).

Every now and then I would go to church with my mother on Sunday, but most of the time I went with Daddy to Zion Hope.

After Mama died I always went to church with Daddy. Once Daddy moved to Rochester I still would go to Sunday school by myself.

I would walk ten blocks to Sunday school every Sunday until I moved away from Sanford to Rochester. These were the times when neighbors would see me Sundays, walking alone, going to church, and they would try to get the low-down on what was happening at 419. As I have shared with you we partied all the time in that house!

Whenever we were asked we were supposed to say, "All is well." That was all the neighborhood people could get out of any of us. "All is well!"

I went to Sunday school so much that I became the Youth Superintendent. I went every Sunday because I enjoyed Sunday school and learning about the Bible, even at this young age.

Sunday school has always been the "meat" of the church for me. Sunday school was a place where different members could express their opinions on what we were reading.

Members could ask questions and get an answers right then. This could not happen in Morning service when the preacher was bringing the message of the day. Sunday school was always good for me because I would come up with some weird questions to ask. At least I thought they were weird!

At that time I was still in high school and I did not know how to tie a necktie. Once I had a tie tied, I would slip it off, over my head, and hang it up tied.

I remember many Sunday mornings I would have to go next door and ask Mr. Robert Herrings to tie my tie for me. Mr. Robert had been drinking all weekend, and would be sleeping on the couch at his house. I would wake him up and have to smell his alcohol breath while he tied my tie. That was the price I had to pay to get my tie tied! Then off to Sunday school I would go! I was in the U.S. Army before I learned to tie a tie.

I remember working in the church with Rev. Brooks, the pastor. At Easter we would always have the Easter egg hunt for the younger children on the Monday after Easter. The older children would boil the eggs and color them. Then, before the little children came to the church, we would go outside and hide the eggs all over the church grounds.

Of course we would eat some of the eggs before we hid them! We would then help the smaller children find the eggs we had hidden. The Easter egg hunt was a lot of fun! I loved anything that had to do with Sunday school.

I was always on the team that planned the "Summer Picnic," as we called it then. We don't use that word (picnic) anymore. We call it the "Summer Outing" now, or the "Church Cookout." There is some strange history around that word "Picnic."

I am now 67 years old and I still love Sunday school. I still try to attend Sunday school every Sunday. I currently teach in the Men's class at Aenon Missionary Baptist Church. But I tie my own ties now!

My current pastor tells me that I have to stay for Morning service to get the full impact of the day celebrating our relationship with God!

Many times in the morning when I am tying my tie for work, or for church, I think about Mr. Robert Herring! Thank you Mr. Robert!

Whenever I go home to Sanford I always visit my old church. Daddy was buried by that church. Aunt "Liza" was buried by that church. Uncle Wilmer was buried by that church, and I always visit there when I'm in Sanford.

Chapter Three

The US Army-My Military Experiences

I was living in Rochester, N.Y. when I received an invitation from Uncle Sam, and he said, "I Want You!" I was working at Rochester General Hospital. I had been there almost a full year.

I was inducted into the Armed services in Buffalo, New York on June 6, 1966. I was shipped to Fort Dix, New Jersey where I went through "Basic Training."

Here are some of my recollections from basic training:

Thinking that I would be rejected for service because of my asthma: I could not walk two city blocks without losing my breath. At the time I was living with my sister Betty, and I had to walk two city blocks to Allene's house for a ride to work. By the time I walked from Betty's to *"Tots"* (as we called her) I would be out of breath.

I did not suffer from asthma as a child in Sanford, but once I moved to Rochester it hit me hard.

I thought I would get out of going to the Army because of it, but that was not the case.

The first three days I was in basic training we had to run one mile every morning. Recruits were passing out every day. It seemed to me that the drill sergeants loved it. The fourth morning I passed out. I thought I was going to die. They took me to the barracks to rest that day, and I never had asthma again. The Army ran it out of me!

There came a day during basic training when we all had to go through the gas chamber. All of the big guys who, up to that point, had dominated the smaller guys, came out of that chamber crying like little babies. Their macho image was destroyed.

Everything in the Army was done by alphabetical order, so being a "C," I went in the chamber and was out. By the time the Ms, Ns, and Ws, etc. came out, I had laughed until I cried a second time. ...because everybody cries from that gas! That's the reason it is called "Tear Gas."

A group of 12 men went into the chamber together. All of us would be wearing our gas masks. We would all wait in the chamber a while to make sure that the masks were working properly. The drill sergeant would then say, "Masks off!" We would all remove our masks, and then, one by one, say our name, rank, and ID number. After this we were allowed to exit the chamber.

The men were called upon alphabetically (from A to Z), using their last names. Everyone else in the group had to hold their breath while the men in front of them "did their thing" and got out!

It would be a sad situation if someone forgot their ID number: the people behind them had to wait.

Someone in each group always forgot their ID number and that guy would get it from the men who were behind him! This was 1966 so there were no females training with us. Everyone had to go through the chamber.

The gas chamber was one of the worst things in basic training!

The day when one of the sergeants made me and another recruit dig a four foot by four foot hole (in the sand) looking for two cigarette butts. This same sergeant had made us bury those butts an hour earlier. He had us dig up the butts because he had forgot to ask us what brand of cigarettes we were smoking.

The two of us were walking back from the Post store, and we were smoking cigarettes. The sergeant saw us throw the butts on the ground. That was a bad thing to do on a Military post. He called us out and said, "...I know you "Shit Birds" did not do what I thought I saw you do?" So he made us dig a hole and bury the butts. Then he asked us what brand did we smoke? We both told that fool, but he wanted to see the butts! We had to start digging again, looking for those butts.

We never found the butts but that was a lesson for us not to throw butts on the ground at the post. Then he made us "low-crawl" back to the barracks, almost a city block in length, on our bellies.

The day we went to the firing range. There was a young man who was having a rough time in basic training. It seemed that he could not do anything right! His fellow recruits picked at him and the sergeants picked at him but I knew something was with this kid, so I did not say anything to him.

I felt sorry for him because everybody picked at him. There was something about his eyes!

At the range the instructor did not know the trainees in our platoon, so he asked for a volunteer to fire the first rounds to prove to us that the bullets were real. Before we knew it that boy who had been picked on had that weapon, was pulling the trigger, and was turning in the direction of the sergeants.

The instructor was still close enough to him to cause the shots to go up into the air. They arrested him and we never saw him again. I believe that if that instructor had not been close enough to stop that young man, he would have killed a lot of people that day.

There was another young man who never was on time for reveille. He was always crying and talking about going home. He never could do anything he was asked.

I thought I hated being there but this was very different! That young man was an accident waiting to happen.

All through basic training I was called "Sad Sack" because I did not want to be in the Army, and everyone knew it. I did not shine my boots, my fatigues was always wrinkled and sometimes not even clean.

I felt bad, I looked bad, and I performed badly. I wanted out, and I had just started.

I had never been away from my family members before, and hated the fact that I was forced to be in the Army.

I tried every trick in the book to get those people to let me go home. The Army today will send a recruit home if he fails to comply with the basic training. This was not the case in the mid-sixties. Back then either you got it right the first eight weeks, or you went through basic training again!

There was this young man from Los Angeles that looked a lot like me, or I looked a lot like him. They always said there is a person somewhere in the world that looks just like you. I found mine in basic training. Some of the other fellows used to call us the twins.

One weekend his girlfriend was coming to the post to visit him. We decided that we would try to fool her. When she got out of the taxi cab I went running up to her, and she did not see that I was the wrong person until I got right in her face. The three of us laughed for a long time. She thought we looked a lot alike too! After basic training I never saw that fellow again.

There were many Sunday mornings when the mess hall was slow, and we would go for breakfast. We would have a contest to see who could eat the most pancakes or eggs. I won the contest on fried eggs that were cooked over easy one morning. I ate 14 eggs that morning. The cook would only give us three at a time, and you could go back as many times as you wished. We had money bet on those contests too.

The Army was not all bad, but, during that time, I just did not want to be there. I missed my family because I had never been away from them for so long.

After "Basic Training" I was shipped to Fort Monroe, Virginia. I spent six months there working with the groundskeeper's platoon. Our responsibilities were to cut grass and care for the grounds of the whole fort. The incident that stands out foremost in my mind from Fort Monroe is when I almost cut off my foot with a lawn mower. I still have the scar! Actually groundskeeping was easy work for me because my father had taught me all about taking care of grounds growing up.

I remember me and one of my fellow servicemen had completed cutting grass on a section of the post for that day. We were on our way back to clean and put the machines away.

He was walking in front of me, pulling his mower behind him. I was walking behind him and his mower. He said something funny and he stopped to laugh.

—

I did not stop and stuck my foot into his mower. I can still hear that mower cutting through my boot. I knew what a lawn mower could do because I used to cut grass to make money as a young fellow. My father had taught me the ins and outs of cutting grass. The incident happened so quickly that I felt nothing, but I knew that something bad had happened.

That mower cut through my boot and my foot. I was out of commission for some time.

I also remember the good times we had on weekend passes, as we visited Richmond, Virginia, and all the towns between. I had really started to enjoy myself!

After my six months' stay at Fort Monroe I was shipped to Baumholder, Germany with the 249th Construction Engineer Battalion. We were support to the 8th Infantry.

Baumholder was on top of a mountain, and it stayed cold year-round. If we were lucky we would see 70 degrees once or twice in August, the rest of the time the temperature was well below 40 degrees.

I drove a ten wheel dump truck. We built things. We tore things down. We built roads, and we paved them over again. I helped mix and pour enough concrete to last me a lifetime.

When I was discharged out of the service my brother-in-law worked in construction. He told me he could get me a job. Construction was the last thing I wanted to do!

These are some of the things that happened during my stay in Germany:

I met my first real White friend. His name was Joseph Jearcco and he was from New York City. He was an Italian. We met on the train from Frankfort to Baumholder. Joe fitted right in with the brothers, and he became one of us. We used to call him JJ. He would always use the threat that "He would go and get his brothers (meaning the Blacks)" if he had any trouble with the other White boys.

Joe would spend most of his time with the Black troops. He would fight with us, eat with us, and always try to get assignments with the brothers.

None of the other groups would mess with him because they all knew he was one of us.

I remember when the company commander caught one of the soldiers asleep guarding the ammo dump. The ammo dump is where the live ammo is stored. When you were on guard duty, you were given three live rounds of ammo. If anyone approached and failed to give the proper password (and you had not been informed that someone was coming), you were to shoot.

This soldier was caught sleeping on guard duty, and he received an article 15. The company commander wanted to warn all of us that he would be checking to see if we were doing the job right. He asked me if I had anything to add? (I think he had heard from someone what I had said what I would do in that situation. I had said, "If I caught an officer climbing over the fence at the ammo dump that is where they would find him!")

The soldier should not have been asleep on guard duty, but that officer should not have been climbing over that fence either!

Once I accepted the fact that I was going to have to do my time, I started to soldier. My boots were shining, my fatigues were sharp, and I was on the ball. I got my entrepreneurial spirit back and started to "Loan Shark." Loan sharking was illegal and you could go to jail for doing it, but it was easy money as long as you did not get caught.

Many of my fellow soldiers had wives and children back home so that is where all of their money went. Many of them just had bad spending habits, and the money ran out long before the end of the month. These men needed to borrow money from someone, ...why not me?! At one point I was making more money than the "First Shirt" loan sharking. I was sending money home to my sister to keep for me until I got out. I was getting a tailor made suit every month. I did very well until I stopped.

Someone might ask, "What could a loan shark do if somebone did not pay?" Easy. That person would be reported to the other loan sharks and that person could not borrow money from anyone. There was a loan shark in every barracks. On some occasions the person who failed to pay back a loan would have an "accident." It has happened!

The company commander was from Rochester, and when it was close to time for me to come home he called me into the office and told me he knew I was loan sharking. He told me I was getting "short" (meaning I was getting close to going home) and that I should stop. I stopped!

They used to have some helluva card games going on around Baumholder. A man could win quite a bit of money just betting on the side, and never handle the cards or the dice. That was my specialty: betting on the side! I won a lot of money betting on the side of card games and dice games. They would say, "Caldwell you want to play?" I would respond, "I am already playing,...and winning!"

Each February we would go to the Rhine River. We were construction engineers and we had to build a pontoon bridge across the Rhine, drive a large crane across it, and then take the bridge down again. The Rhine River was about one half mile across and it flowed about eight miles per hour. This exercise was done to keep us ready to perform a task like this for the 8th Infantry, their tanks, trucks and soldiers, if need be.

This exercise meant a week of sleeping in tents, and performing our tasks on the move. There were men on the ground putting together the large pontoons. There were men constructing the metal planks that were strapped to the pontoons. There were men floating the pieces out into the river connecting everything together. We constructed the bridge twenty feet at a time across the river. Another company of engineers on the other side would be working towards us. It took us three and one half days to complete the bridge, and one and one half days to take it down.

One day about twenty men were taking a completed section of bridge out on the river to connect it. Too many men were on one side of it and the section tipped over. Those men were spread up and down that river so quickly that it was quite a fright!

As I mentioned the Rhine flowed at 8 miles per hour! Luckily all of the men had on their life jackets, and the speed boats picked them up safely in about 20 minutes.

I had some great pictures of all of those red life jackets spread all over the Rhine, but over the years the pictures have been misplaced. I told my first sergeant that I wanted to work on land, and not on any boat, or anything on the water!

While we were building the bridge across the Rhine River we had to sleep in tents on the ground. It was cold and we were told every day to wash our feet and keep them dry. There was this young man who did not do a good job of that and his toes froze.

The fellow lost two toes from one of his feet. We all felt bad for him, but he got to go home and recuperated in an American hospital. We never saw him again.

Getting letters from home was always a sign that a man had good home support. I got a letter from my then girlfriend every other day. I got a package of goodies from my friend and sister *"Cat"* every two weeks. The guys knew when my packages were coming and they were always ready.

My first sergeant used to come to me to get homemade peanut brittle that my sister would send. I remember when a fellow soldier would get a "Dear John" letter from home, and how cruel the jokes would be for a week or two until someone else would get one. "Dear John" letters were letters a girlfriend or wife would write telling the enlisted man that they would wait no longer. There were fights and suicides too when men received these letters!

There was this White fellow from Virginia who received a "Dear John" letter from home, and that poor man cried for a month. The other fellows did not give him anything but trouble.

I remember when I was learning how to drive those big dump trucks, I was scared to death. I had never driven anything so large, and it was quite a learning experience. There were two people in the trucks all the times. One day I was driving, and Willie Williams from Richmond, Virginia was riding what we called "shotgun."

We were going down one of those mountains in Germany and I was unable to downshift. The truck kept going down that hill, and we could see a curve coming up fast. I am trying to gear down and nothing was happening. As we reached the curve I finally was able to shift down, ...but it was too late. I thought the truck was going too fast to jump out but Willie did not feel that way and out he went, just before we went into that curve. I was stuck with the truck and it got caught by the guardrail.

By the time the truck had come to a full stop, it was rocking on a 300 ft. drop, held there by the guardrail. I got out to see what had happen, about the same time Williams had run about a half mile down the hill to see too. He said, "I thought you were a dead man! I got out of that damn truck!" He used other words!

When he said that I saw how close I was to going over that cliff. Now I became scared, my knees started to shake, as I realized how close I had come to certain death.

I remember how we used to behave in the mess hall, where everybody went to eat. One of the first things I learned was to become good friends with the cooks. Most of the cooks were brothers so we could always get something to eat, and we could get away with cutting the line because the cooks were our friends.

At meal time the line would be going out of the door and 8 to 10 of the brothers (with JJ in the middle) would just walk in the mess hall. We would go up to the front of the line, get our trays, get our food, sit and eat. The other soldiers would complain but no one would do anything... so it continued.

One day a group of soldiers decided that enough was enough, and we were not cutting the line that day. Oh! A fight broke out, and it was on! The place was turned out! I was never much for fighting (and would avoid it if I could). This day though I was right in the middle of it.

I grabbed this little White boy who had started the protest.

He looked small enough, and I felt I could take him easily. **Wrong!** I grabbed him, hit him in the mouth as hard as I could, spent him around, and threw him into the wall face first.

That skinny little White boy bounced off of the wall and started hitting me so fast I could not see his hands!

I was covering up, trying to protect my face, and he kept coming.

I was looking for some help from somewhere, but none came. Everyone was busy looking out for themselves. Oh, by the way, we stopped cutting the line for a month or so. After that it did continue but never as bold as we had gotten before. JJ was "in the mix," and got his share of that melee too.

At some point, when I was enlisted, French President De Gaulle decided to expel the USA out of France. The United States had military bases all over France. There had been some kind of misunderstanding between the two countries and the USA was out!

Since we were construction engineers we were assigned the task of going to Paris and dismantling several buildings there, and bringing all of the construction materials back to Germany. We were on what was called "TDY" (temporary duty). Close to 60 men from our battalion were sent to Paris for three months. This was great duty! The party was on!

Every one of the young military men (with lots of money and plenty to spend it on) had the time of our lives for three months. Some of those men that were sent were shopping for girls like candy in the candy shop.

There were many times we would save up our leave time to spend a week in Sweden. This was a great time in my life. I was so thankful that I had not been sent to Viet Nam. Thank God!

Many of the men who came to Germany were coming from Viet Nam to complete their tour of duty. They would tell us that we were in heaven doing our time in Germany. There were some guys that wanted to be fighting, so they volunteered to go to Viet Nam, but not Fred!

One of the things that happened when I was in Germany was that the US troops and the German troops worked together training dogs.

These were war dogs, and guard dogs for the ammunition storage areas.

This joint effort gave the US troops and the German troops an opportunity to train together. The US troops were chosen as we stood in formation. The dogs were brought close to each one of us. The dogs were friendly to some of us and growled at others. I was one of the ones that the dogs growled at. The work we were assigned to do was decided by the dogs.

I learned that some people have an odor that upsets dogs. From our company me and another soldier named James Long upset the dogs whenever we got close to them. We were then trained how to aggravate the dogs.

The primary soldier who trained with a particular dog would take the dog through its daily paces. Usually all would go very well. Then, me, Long, and some other German troops who had "the smell" would tease the dogs and get them aggravated and angry.

Then the dogs would be taken through their paces in an aggravated state. If they performed well angry and upset they were deemed "good dogs." If they failed to perform satisfactorily they would be removed from the program.

James Long and I were the best at getting the dogs perturbed and upset. I can't tell you the things we would do to those dogs. They hated us something fierce!

My experiences with these war and guard dogs is one of the reasons I do not approach dogs that I am not familiar with: I have that smell.

I will not go into homes if the owner will not shut their dogs away. There are a lot of people who say, "Come on in, he (or she) won't bite." I know better!

When I see people walking their dogs I always cross the street to the other side.

Finding out that I had "that smell" was very strange for me because I had worked with dogs in some way all my life. I never knew I had that kind of impact on them until I was in the Army.

These dogs were trained to perform in war situations, and on patrol at the ammo dumps. These animals were trained to obey hand signals, and to react/respond to verbal commands also. My exposure to these animals while in the Army was a great learning experience and gave me a great foundation for my work in the animal research lab at Rochester General.

Chapter Four

Life Mentors

My Friend and Mentor - Daddy Melvin Mc Cray

I met Daddy Melvin in Rochester, New York when my first wife and I, and our four children, were living at 6 Leopold Street. He and "Mrs. Pearl" (as we called her) lived across the street in front of us. He was about 69 or 70 years old when we met.

My wife and her family had lived on Leopold Street for many years. After we were married I moved into the house and my wife's mother moved out and gave us the house.

God bless my first mother-in-law!

I had seen the old man and his wife, and how well they interacted with the neighbors on the street. Mrs. Pearl would baby sit for all of the young parents working and getting started in life.

Daddy Melvin and I really hit it off when he found out that I had joined the Masons. He was an old Mason from way back, and was well versed on the subject. He became my teacher, and I learned so much from him about life, the Bible, and Masonry.

Of course I never knew he was a Mason until he approached me, because he never said anything to me, other than the normal greetings. Why would he?

He used to wait for me to come home from work in the evening and meet me at my car with a question, and a lecture. He would hit me with a question as soon as I got home. Then he would walk away as he spoke, and I would follow because I was so interested... and he knew it!

I loved it because it put me so far ahead of the other young men who had joined the Masons at the same time as I had.

After a while he decided to reinstate in the same lodge I was in. He then became the teacher of all of us. This man had been a member of every secret order that a Black man could join. He was well versed in the Bible, and could mix the two disciplines well. The entire lodge loved him and learned so much from him. But he was mine because he lived across the street from me. I received some training from him every day, and all weekend.

A few of us used to go over to his house every week to study, and hear the old man talk about Masonry, the Bible, and life.

We would gather around that old pot belly stove he had. Mama Pearl would go into the next room so that we could talk freely, and Daddy Melvin would start to teach.

He told us he had gathered all of the information he was sharing over the years and had no one to share it with. Now that he had several young men seeking this information it excited him to no end. He would talk late into the night but we had to go home because we had to go to work the next day. He said that he did not want to die and take all of the information he had gathered to the grave: he would rather leave it here with us.

I thank God that Daddy Melvin found me to teach! He has a lot to do with the man I am today.

I later learned that he was from Sanford, Florida, my hometown too! Daddy Melvin was twenty five years older than his wife, and they had moved to Rochester from Sanford many years ago.

Up until the time I got to know Daddy Melvin he had never talked about his living in Sanford. I guess it was a part of his life he wanted to forget.

There was a lady in Sanford we kids used to call "Jump Little Rabbit." She was one of the town drunks. We used to tease her and laugh at her when she *"put on a show"* all over town.

One year when we were coming North to work the season Jump Little Rabbit (Mrs. Louise Burton was her given name), and my sister Verdene took care of all of the young teenagers by preparing our meals and feeding us. She was a nice woman. She just drank a lot.

The story was that she had lost her mind when her husband had left her for a younger woman and then had left town.

Come to find out (after I gotten to know Daddy Melvin better) that he was that man, and Mama Pearl was that younger woman.

All of the young people called Daddy Melvin and Mrs. Pearl, "Mama" and "Daddy."

I remember as a child in Sanford that there was a little man who rode a bicycle all over town. Many times I had seen him on that bike. He had coon tails on the handle bars and a little horn that he "beeped, beeped" when he went by. I had seen my father talking to him but I never knew the two men were one in the same until I got to know him here in Rochester.

Daddy Melvin used to walk to the store to get supplies for his house. He was a little man and an old man walking down the street alone might seem like prey.

Early one morning he was going to the store and some young men (three of them) saw him and crossed over the street to the side he was walking. He felt that they were thinking about doing something to him. Daddy Melvin said to himself, "Not today!"

He reached into his pocket and took out his little .22 caliber pistol and raised it high in the air so that they could see it clearly. Daddy Melvin said those young men crossed back over to the other side of the street just as cool as they had crossed over in the first place.

He did not crack a smile as he told that story. He said he wanted them to be sure of what they were doing. We laughed so hard some of us cried, but Daddy said it was not funny. He said he was ready to kill them all that day!

Daddy Melvin said, "As you walk along the road of life and you see a fool sitting on the curb crying, don't stop and talk to that person.

You may call out to them and say, "Get up, we must keep moving along the road of life." But he told us that you must never stop and talk to them.

If you stop and talk to them, the next person walking along the road of life will see two fools sitting on the curb crying.

He was one of the best instructors I have ever studied under.

When we would go to other cities for Masonic meetings Daddy Melvin would travel with us. Once we got to the city we were going to Daddy Melvin would say, "Okay boys, find the drug store so the old man can get his prescription filled." He was referring to the liquor store so we could get him something to drink.

We would attend the meetings during the day, and would listen to Daddy Melvin tell stories all night of his very interesting life. He used to tell us stories about when he rode the rails form the West coast to the East coast. This man had played piano in little honky tonks all across the country. We would invite other brothers from other cities to our room, and they loved him too!

On the occasions when Daddy Melvin was not feeling well and did not travel with us those other brothers would ask where he was, and how he was doing.

Daddy Melvin was quite the drinker, and he would always have a little bottle in his pocket. There were times when he would be so ill that he had to be hospitalized. We would all go to visit him in our Masonic uniforms, and he would love it.

Mrs. Pearl would see ten or twelve young men coming all dressed up and she would start crying. Daddy Melvin would say "Hush woman, those are our children."

He would tell us how well he was treated by the hospital staff after they saw all of us come to visit him dressed in our Masonic uniforms.

It was strange but Daddy Melvin would do better when he was drinking, because every time he tried to quit, he got sick. So we would always have something for him to drink. The doctor had told him several times that if he did not quit drinking he would die. Daddy Melvin said he had to die from something, it might as well be something he enjoyed doing.

Daddy Melvin would always say get the question right before you think about what the answer should be.

Daddy Melvin used to tell us, "You never have to back up any further than your book." If you had a disagreement with someone about what the book said, go to the book! If that person still disagrees with you, he is now disagreeing with the book. Only a fool argues with the book! If you continue to argue with that person then there are two fools arguing.

He taught us principles about keeping the peace. Even if it meant shutting up when you were right.

Daddy Melvin died at the age of 86, and his mind was as sharp as a twenty-five year old man. He knew the Masonic ritual from cover to cover by memory. He could tell you what page to go to for any answer in that book. He also knew the Bible very well and could transform the story into words where you could see what he was talking about. He was a great teacher!

He said that once you make up your mind to do a job, it was half done. The hard part is making up your mind!

"Mrs. Pearl" Mc Cray

Mrs. Pearl was a big woman. She stood about 6'3" and she weighed close to 400 lbs. Daddy Melvin was a little man about 5'6 and did not weigh 100 lbs. with his clothes wet. They were a loving couple, and everybody who knew them loved them.

Mrs. Pearl always said that she wanted to die first because she did not know what she would do without him. He died first, and she died several years after.

We used to take her to church in a double wide wheelchair when she got so she could not walk anymore. We had to bury her in a double wide casket.

Daddy Melvin used to say about Mrs. Pearl, "She may not look good to you, but she look real good to me!

He was truly my friend, and my teacher.

We used to take him to the lakeside in the morning so he could fish. After work we would go back and pick him up, and he would have a large catch of fish for all to eat that day. We would clean those fish and Mrs. Pearl would cook them.

I would buy several slabs of pork ribs, give them to Daddy Melvin and Mrs. Pearl, and they would have dinner ready when we got home that day. The dinner they prepared was for several families in the neighborhood. There were about twenty houses on each side of the street, and everyone knew each other.

Daddy Melvin would eat a little, Mrs. Pearl would eat one whole slab, and the neighborhood would eat the rest. Those were some great days!

Another man from Sanford, Florida who had settled in Rochester (Rev. Pringle) started a prayer band in Daddy Melvin and Mrs. Pearl's home when they were living on Ward Street. That prayer band ended up being a church on Grand Avenue.

They were just a great set of people. We had both their funerals in that church on Grand Ave. That church is now pastored by one of our lodge brothers!

My Friend and Mentor James "MAMBA" McCuller

I was working at Rochester General Hospital. Every day after work I would go home, sit and play music, and go to work the next day. This was not the kind of life I wanted to live. Eventually a friend told me that ABC (Action for a Better Community, Inc.) was looking for volunteers. I volunteered.

I met James McCuller when I started volunteering for ABC. ABC is a community action agency in Rochester, NY.

I wanted to do something in the community, so I was asked by a friend to join the steering committee of ABC.

The steering committee was a group of 45 community people who had to get other community people to sign a petition so they could run in a community wide election in order to serve on the ABC steering committee.

Of these 45 people the top 15 vote getters would then serve on the "Board of Directors" of ABC. After their term was served the process was done again. This happened every two years.

I was one of the top vote getters for about four years running, and then I was number 16 and could not sit on the board. I was not happy about that, and neither was James McCuller. James was the Executive Director of ABC and we had done some good work together. I had learned a great deal from him about community action, and I wanted to continue learning.

I was working at Rochester General Hospital, so James went to the President of RGH and asked him to establish a seat on ABC's board and allow me to sit in it. Mr. Leighbert agreed, and now RGH had a seat on ABC's board of directors which Freddie Caldwell could sit in.

Mr. Leighbert said that I could serve with the one condition that I could not make decisions for the hospital. That was fine with me and Jim. Now I did not have to go through the election process every two years. Now I was James' to train as he pleased, and train he did.

One of the lessons he taught us was "Documentation! Documentation! Documentation!" "Document your Documentation with Documentation!"

I learned so much about community action that after fifthteen years I was ready to serve as ABC board president. I held that position for seven years.

The first two years on the board I went to every meeting and listened only. I was learning. One of the things that fascinated me about this organization was that it touched your life from conception to your death.

James "MAMBA" McCuller was one of the greatest public speakers I have ever heard. He could hold the attention of an audience, and keep them on the edge of their seats for his entire presentation. I would put him up against anyone who ever did it. I would put my money on Jim against any public speaker of your choice.

Jim was a show off and he knew he was good. He would always travel with a large group of people: "The Entourage "we called it. I was always ready to follow him anywhere! He was that kind of leader, and many people in Rochester would attest to that fact.

Jim was one of those people who could read a book over the weekend, and teach from that book on Monday. He had that kind of mind. I would have to read that book several times, and then study it before I could teach from it. This was a gift the man had!

As a volunteer at ABC, and having experience working at the hospital, Jim would always give me the work that dealt with healthcare. So in the early 80's when we began learning about HIV and AIDS that became my area.

We went to Attica State Correctional Facility (Attica, NY) to speak with the warden to find out if we could provide education for the inmates on HIV and AIDS. We had learned that prison was a breeding ground for the disease.

The warden told us, "Doesn't any sex go on in here!"

Jim stood up and said, "OK folks this meeting is over." We stood up, and walked out!

After some time we received permission from Attica to let us come in and provide HIV and AIDS education for the inmates. I think the warden changed his mind when he found this was a growing practice across the country. Can you believe a warden of a prison would say such a thing?

When he started the "Black Men Study Group" he told us that we could be called Dr. in the group when we could document that we had read 100 books. To this group PHD meant books Piled High & Deep. We would have to write a summary of the book we had read with author and highlights of the book. We read and discussed a lot of books. It took me three years to complete mine, but I did. Then he started calling me Dr. Caldwell, or Dr. Kuumba, which is my chosen African name.

In this group you could have an African name of your choice, or the members of the group would find one for you. The name had to fit your personality, and have in it a charge for your life.

My chosen name was "Kuumba" from the seven principles of the NGUZO SABA by Dr. Maulana Karenga.

"Kuumba" means, "I will do all I can, in any way I can, to leave my community more beautiful and beneficial than it was when I inherited it".

Jim got sick all of a sudden as it seems, and the next thing I knew he was in the hospital. Then he died!

While he was in the hospital I went to see him, and he told me he was not coming back to work. I told him it was the medication making him talk that way. I was mistaken!

One day when I went to visit him in the hospital he was talking about the ABC board finding the best person we could to take his place. "Just put the best person you can find in my seat to take the agency he had built into the future".

Then he started talking about the TV program we were watching. One of those fishing shows where they catch the fish and then put them back into the water. He thought that was the worst thing in the world. He said they should put that fish in some hot grease, with some onions and have a feast.

Jim said those guys fish for sport. When poor people fish it is for support! We laughed and laughed! That was the last time I saw him alive!

He died a few weeks later! I lost a good friend, and I lost a great teacher!

I remember when he took us with him to do a speaking engagement at Attica State Prison. There had to be about 40 of us traveling with him that day. We took one of the Head Start buses and filled it with staff and volunteers of the agency. I had never been inside a prison before, and Jim told us that we should be afraid.

We were allowed into one area, and the door closed behind us. Then another door opened, we were allowed through that door, then it closed. Then a voice came over the loudspeaker and said, "You are in a controlled area!" That is when we knew it was real.

We went through the screening procedure and were escorted to this large hall full of inmates.

Jim's topic was "Excellent, Not Perfect." As he spoke every now and then he would have the inmates yell out loud, "Excellent but not perfect!"

Each time the inmates would get louder and louder! The guards were getting a little concerned as to how the inmates were getting into the presentation. Then one of the lead guards stepped up front and brought everything to a close. They accused Jim of inciting a riot. They rounded us up and escorted us out of the prison.

When we entered the prison they would search us to make sure there were no weapons, or contraband going inside. Jim used to say his greatest weapon was his mouth, and they can't send me in without that!

Jim said, "Think about it! Whenever visitors from the outside entered the prison they would be searched from their head to their feet. Whenever the guards would enter the prison going to work they would just walk in carrying their bags and coats, etc. Now you tell me how contraband gets into the prison!"

Jim went to the prison (Attica) to speak many times, and he would always start his presentation with this opening: "I bring you greetings from the incarcerated on the outside, to the incarcerated on the inside. We know you are here, and we want you to know you are loved, and cared for by those you left back home."

I remember once we were in Albany, NY for a community action conference and Jim was the keynote speaker. He was about half way into his presentation and a lady upfront had a heart attack. Jim did not miss a beat. The lady was hurriedly taken to the hospital and the presentation went on as if nothing had happen. The applause he received was not only for the great presentation, but for the way he handled the situation. It was so cool! I was so proud of him that day.

Jim McCuller was the best friend any poor person ever had. He considered poor people his responsibility and he taught us to think the same way.

There were times when I went into his office to discuss some issue, and Jim had a way of making you feel you were the only person in the world. He would listen to you very intently, formulating an answer as you spoke. He would then make sure he understood what you were saying, and then give you several answers to your concern. Then he would say if you take this option, this is what will happen. Or if you take another option this would happen.

He just had a way about him, and we all tried to immitate him as closely as we could. I know I did!

I remember one time when I was doing so well with the Cultural Diversity Education at RGH that the city asked me to do some city wide work in this area. I took Jim out to lunch for advice. He simply told me to do what I thought best, but remember it is not how much money you make, but how long you make money.

This meant that in politics you work as long as your man or woman is in office, then you are unemployed. I concluded that this meant for me to stay at the hospital and make that small money for a long time. I thought he was saying if I quit the hospital and went to work for the city to make a lot of money for four years (maybe), that I would live to regret it.

When this happened I had been working at the Rochester General Hospital for twenty or so years. I retired after forty years. This may not have happened if I left. I will always be thankful to him for the advice.

I remember Jim nominated me for the Jefferson Award. I thought it was so cool that he did that.

He told the audience that he was aggressively effective in the work he did. He told them that I was passively effective in the way I did my work. He was nominating me because he felt I was effective, and that is what counted.

He used to tell me that I was like my mother, passive. He wanted me to be more like my father, aggressive. We knew each other that well because in the Black men's study group, the members got to know one another that well. We would talk about all aspects of our lives.

Jim McCuller was quite a golfer. He took me with him to the driving range, and I watched him hit some balls. He tried to get me to play the game, but I was not ready.

Now, the annual golf outing that ABC sponsors is named in his honor!

When I went to the range with him the drives were consistently going about 275 – 300 yards. I did not know at that time what a great drive 300 yards represented! It was not the time for me and golf.

Jim suggested that I get some cheap used clubs just to see if I would like the game. I was not ready!

My Friend & Mentor James H. Norman

I met James Norman when we were looking for a person to carry the agency (ABC) into the future after Jim McCuller had died. Mr. Norman was one of 108 people who applied for the position.

The agency decided to use ABC staff, community leaders, and the board of directors to constitute the team that would hire the new Executive Director.

We had to develop a process because we thought we would always have Jim McCuller as our leader.

The process was for the team to use resumes to cut the 108 applicants in half. Then we would do the same thing to cut that number in half again. At this time there were about 50 applicants left. We cut it in half again, and started to interview the last 25 applicants. James Norman was in the lead all the way through the process.

We then interviewed the last 25, and asked the top 12 to come back for a second interview. James Norman was one of those also.

I was asked to escort him out after his first interview. He was having some trouble getting back for the date and time of his second interview. As we walked out I assured him that it would be to his advantage to make sure he was there for the next interview. I knew he was the leading candidate but he was not aware of that fact! He assured me he would, and he did.

I think we were becoming friends at that time!

As we had worked our way through the interview process we had come to know each other quite well. I was thinking about what Jim McCuller had told me: "Put the best person you can find in my seat!"

Jim McCuller had died in April 1992, and we hired James Norman by November 1992. I will always believe that God was in this process all the way through.

I was the vice president of the board of directors, and chairman of the search committee. Soon it was time for me to become the president of the board. I felt good because I had James to guide, and assist me.

He is a great teacher, and allowed me to grow at a rate that was right for me. He helped me to understand community action in a new way. Helping people to help themselves is a wonderful thing once you get the hang of it.

I was working at RGH all the time I was board president. I served as president for seven years. I was director of Cultural Diversity Initiatives at RGH. We had developed a training program that was getting recognition across the community.

I felt at the time that there were too many White people at RGH for the training to be effective. We needed some diversity in the training. So we spoke to ABC and Ibero American Action League to involve their staff in the education. This was a win-win situation for all involved: RGH could now provide a worthwhile training for its staff and ABC and Ibero could get their staff trained in cultural diversity for free. Everybody benefited. It was great! We took over two thousand people through that experience, and everybody enjoyed it. Well almost everybody! I still get compliments today about that training.

Then as we tried to make it better, which required more risk on RGH's part the training slowed to a stop. James found out I was looking for something else and invited me to work for him and with him as staff at ABC. I was so happy I did not know what to do.

I worked for ABC for five years, the best years of my life. I learned so much and got to work with some great people.

One of the lessons I learned from James was "The Process!" He always said we should develop a process for doing everything. He said if you follow the process and things don't go the way you planned, there is something wrong with the process. If you follow the process things should go the way you planned. If things go wrong you must have not followed the process.

This is the same lesson James McCuller taught when he said plan your work and work the plan, and things should come out fine. They were both right!

Proper Planning Prevents Poor Performance!

James had his executive team reading books that would help us do our jobs. This was a great way to continue our education, and it was job related.

This effort worked just like the reading that we did in the Black Men's study group. Each member of the group had a section to read and then report back to the other members what it meant to them. The same thing happened when James had us to read a book, and discuss what it means. Great learning process!

At the many training conferences staff attended we were always learning new material that would help us do our jobs better.
This one speaker in Chicago said something that has been with me ever since she said it.

She stated that community action agencies across America have the tendency to keep people on payroll long after they have quit working. I did not get it at first, but after a while I got it. Then I started looking for this phenomenon at ABC. Yes, we were guilty too!

I was working at the hospital, and had been there a long time. I had plenty of vacation time in my bank so every time James said, "Do you want to go to a conference with me?" I said let's go!

I followed this man all over the United States learning about community action.

Others had tried to get me interested in playing golf. I had always thought it was a waste of time and it was a White man's game. Then I was introduced to Tiger Woods. James helped me to understand the game and how it could help you think, and relax. Plus it turned out to be a lot of fun!

Of the many trips we took these are the ones I remember most.

James and I went to New Orleans for a conference and I had injured my shoulder. So I could not play any golf. I walked the course with him as he played. So I asked him to think out loud so I could learn how to think the game. We had a great time, and that was one of my most memorable sessions of golf education.

James and I went to a conference in Washington D.C., and I met the man named David Bradley that worked in that city getting money for community action agencies all over America, and its territories.

This was when I learned the great effort men like James and our lobbyist David put forth to assist poor people in this country. This is the trip that really convinced me I was doing the right thing.

At all of these conferences I would attend the sessions that would help me be a good board president. One quote I remember is "Board members are supposed to get the money to run the agency, or get out of the way of others getting the money to run the agency." Funny, but true!

James and I went to a conference in Miami, and I got to see some of my long lost relatives. We also got to play golf on some of the world renowned courses there, and I got another dose of community action.

At these conferences we got to spend time with others from across the country doing the same kind of work. What a great educational process!

In Miami James told me, "If you go to a golf course and look across the playing area and you see no trees, or woods, look out for the sand and the water. Water has always intimidated me on the golf course. We played a course like that in Miami, and I lost 12 balls that day.

Please don't think I can play this game very well, because I can't. I just love to spend time with great people laughing, having fun, and losing balls.

On one occasion James asked me, "Freddie, do you know why your game does not improve?" I responded, "Why?" He said, "Because you don't care....!" He was right! I just love to spend time with people I like! I hit the ball and if I can find it, I hit it again. Sooner or later I will get it to the hole!

James and I went to a conference in Boston. We were there to learn about working better with churches in our community. There were community action people there from all across America. We learned that assisting poor people would go smoother and be a lot simpler if we could involve the churches. There were church leaders there from all over the country too!

Jim McCuller used to say that the shakers and movers are sitting in the church on Sunday morning, and we have to learn how to gain their assistance.

While we were in Boston we played one of the most beautiful, well cared for golf courses I had ever seen. On the first hole James told me not to dig up these people beautiful golf course. On that first hole I took out one of the biggest dibbits I have ever seen. James told the other guys playing with us, "I don't know that guy. He is not traveling with me!"

I said I wanted to leave them something to remember me by. We had a great time out in those woods!

My volunteering with ABC has gotten me to see places I would never have seen if it were not for James allowing me to travel and learn. We were always on an airplane going somewhere, and it amounted to a college education for me. We had suits in one bag, and golf clubs in the other!

Then I went to James to ask a big favor. I had been married two times, and was ready to try it again. I asked him to be my best man for my wedding to my third wife. Without hesitation he said "Yes" and the planning began!

I will always be grateful to James Norman for saying yes to my request. The best man to me meant just that. I will always consider him a great friend for allowing me to come and work, and learn community action under his tutelage. Even though we were close in age he is one of my life mentors.

Chapter Five

My Years at Rochester General Hospital

I graduated from high school on June 7th, 1965 in Sanford, Florida and on July 20th, 1965 I was employed at Rochester General Hospital Westside Division.

I worked in the animal lab with rabbits for pregnancy tests, and guinea pigs for TB testing. In that small lab there were about 6-8 rabbits, and about 30 guinea pigs.

I joined this organization (RGH) when the two hospitals were being consolidated into one. There was a West Side Division, and a North Side Division. I would guess that we had 200 employees at the Westside Division and it had to be moved to the other side of town.

At the North Side Division there were another 500 employees, and in Jan 1966 everyone was working at North Side on 1425 Portland Ave.

I met my first wife in Feb 1966. She was employed in the cafeteria, and I worked in the Charles O. Sailor Research and Clinical Development Laboratory. It was not called that at the time, it was just the animal lab. It was later named after one of the doctors who spent a lot of time working in the developing of surgical technique.

I remember when the construction crews came to the RGH campus in 1968, and they have been building ever since.

I was part of the Department of Surgery & Education headed by a Dr. Raymond Hinshaw. He had the best surgical hands I have ever seen. Over the years we worked on dogs, cats, monkeys, sheep, pigs, and every animal you may find on the farm.

My first memories in the lab at RGH were on Monday of each week we did an open heart surgical procedure on dogs. Open heart surgery was in its infancy, and RGH was right there on the cutting edge.

The people who worked in the lab took care of the animal's needs for food, water, and keeping the cages clean. I had some experience taking care of animals because I took care of my father's hunting dogs back home in Sanford, Florida.

I liked the work, and the man I worked for (Lee Spidel) liked me, so it became a perfect match. He started me in school at the University of Rochester taking courses in Animal Husbandry (the study of Man and animals living in the same enclosed area for the enhancement of Man.)

I went on to the University of Delhi Suny and acquired more education in this field. I liked working in the lab.

In June of 1966 I was drafted into the Army, and returned to RGH in May of 1968. These two years were counted as though I was still there working.

After I came home from the army RGH was not ready to take me back, so I went job hunting. I started working at Rochester Products where they made automobile parts. The money was great but the hours were terrible. I worked from 11pm until 7am. I worked there about four months and RGH had placed me back as an employee in the animal research lab again. For a short time I worked in both places.

I would have kept both jobs but my uncle Wilmer died in Sanford and I wanted to go to the funeral. Rochester Products told me that he was not immediate family, therefore I could not go.

Not the case! This man had helped to raise us when my mother died, and nothing was going to keep me from going. So I went! I also lost that job. Oh well!

Also, I had gotten my real job back at the hospital. RGH was where I really wanted to be. At that time I was also just glad to be out of the Army, and glad to be back home.

My life became wrapped up in my employment. My friends were people I worked with at the hospital. My social life was with the people from the hospital. My first wife and I met at the hospital. We started having babies; both of us trying to go to school, and working two jobs.

This was about the time that Freddie Perry was hired at RGH. He became a lifelong friend and work partner at RGH. The two of us ran the lab for the next thirty years. Freddie P. (as we called him) was also from Sanford, Florida. I was a few years ahead of him in high school and did not get to know him there. But after we both moved to Rochester and started working together, we became the best of friends.

In those days we got a new group of young interns every year. These young doctors in training had ideas about how to improve some surgical technique, and/or create a new technique. Dr. Harrison was the director of our group and he would introduce these doctors to us, and have them explain what they wanted to do.

It was our responsibility to assist them in identifying the appropriate research animal, assist in performing the surgical procedure and the tests, and the collection of the data. If they "got on to something" and it was accepted in the American Medical Journal, their young careers would be off and running. It happened many times at RGH.

I had started off at Monroe Community College (MCC) to become a nurse but soon realized that I could not stand to be around sick people: Old sick people we could do nothing to help; babies crying you could not help. I could not take it! So I used my nursing training in the lab working with animals.

It was my responsibility to oversee the operation of the laboratory. We got the animals in and made sure they were healthy. Then they would be assigned to a research project. We did the pre-op work, the operation or surgery, we did the post-op work. I nursed the animals back to health again.

We called Freddie Perry the "General Surgeon" because he had very good surgical hands, and he loved doing surgery.

I, on the other hand, hated to do surgery, and preferred doing the pre-op and post-op work. We made a perfect team. Perry would assist the doctor in performing the research surgical procedure once or twice, and from then on Perry could do it. That is why we called him the general surgeon. He used to walk around with a lab coat with General Surgeon written on it.

Dr. Howard Harrison was the director of our division, and I reported to him. I was the chief animal research technician, and I had two staff people working in the lab with me.

Dr. Harrison was the chief of research and he was a burn specialist. He had two researchers that worked in his lab inside the hospital.

Taking care of the animals over the weekend was overtime, so we had to share the overtime. Myself, two people who worked in the lab with me, and the two researchers who worked for Dr. H. (as we called him) all worked a weekend. This was a total of five people.

Everytime the researchers who worked for Dr. H. worked the weekend (two White boys) the work was not done correctly.

This meant that when my team came in Monday morning we found the animals sometimes had not been fed, the dogs had not been let out so the cages were full of you know what, and the lab was in a mess. This meant extra work for me and my team.

Eventually I confronted them about the weekend work but over time there was no improvement. I decided that it was time for me to report this to Dr. H.

A meeting was scheduled for the four of us to meet and discuss the matter of weekend work. So there we are in Dr. H.'s office, and I am telling him about the "piss-poor" weekend work these two White boys were doing, and the lab team had to do their work on Monday morning.

We talked back and forth for about two hours, and when I left from that office I felt as though I had got the whipping! I felt like I had done something wrong.

The nerve of this Black man, telling another White man, about the inadequacies of two other White men! Such a thing was unheard of in Rochester, NY in the early 1970s. You may want to give it some thought today, but not then!

What a lesson I learned that day. Of course nothing was done, and the problem persisted. The slave telling on the master! You must be crazy Fred!

This is not the way the world works in America. This was in the 1970s. Rochester, NY is still in many ways acting like it is in the 1960s.

We kept the lab so clean you could eat off the floor. We had to because we had to be ready for the federal inspectors at all times. We got no notice, just a knock on the door.

The Federal Inspector worked for the USDA, and they could be very tough. We had this one inspector, a White female, who told the lab to change from cast-iron cages to stainless steel cages, and we had 90 days to comply. (The USDA had told us about the change in regulations and we had notified the leadership at RGH but nothing had happened.)

I took her up to Dr. Harrison's office where she made her request about the cages. Freddie Perry and I would love to have new cages. It would have made our lives a lot better, but the hospital said they had no money for new cages.

Dr. Harrison took her up to Dr. Hinshaw's office where she made her request for the new cages. She told Dr. Hinshaw that she would return in 90 days, and expected to see new cages, or she would close the lab, have us sacrifice (kill) all the animals, send the staff home, and fine the hospital 10 thousand dollars. She could do that, and we all knew it.

Dr. Hinshaw wanted to know where I found an inspector like that? I assured him that she had found us.

Upon her return the hospital had found about 15 thousand dollars and we had gotten new cages. That was the way that went!

There was one occasion when a visiting professor from Buffalo, NY provided surgical training. There were several training sessions going on at the same time. Dr. Hinshaw was the cleanest surgeon I have ever seen. He cleaned the surgical site as he went. There was never a bloody mess when he worked. He was neat and clean from start to finish!

Back in those days there were no fancy machines to perform the surgery. The doctor had to cut into the area he wanted to work in, and then clean and stitch his way out. All of this was done by hand. Dr. Hinshaw's expertise was why he was the Chief of Surgery.

He was a master surgeon!

Dr. Hinshaw was conducting one session in the first OR (operating room), and the visiting professor was conducting another in the second OR. I was observing and assisting the visiting professor, and Freddie Perry was observing and assisting Dr. Hinshaw.

When the workshop was completed I complimented the visiting professor on his surgical technique. I said "You do beautiful work doctor."

He gave me a look that said "Who the hell are you to comment on my work?" He did not say that but his facial expression said it.

He looked me up and down like I was a midget. It was racial. He knew it, and I knew it too.

Then he said, "I guess you have seen enough procedures to judge my work!" This was after about twenty five years watching and assisting doctors do surgery in the surgical developmental laboratory.

This just goes to show you that race is in everything in America. Sometimes it slips in unexpectedly.

I am sure he would have liked to say it another way, but he chose to be respectful.

I worked in that lab for 32 years. After a while the concept of cross-training became popular in the workplace. I crossed-trained in Human Resources (Personnel) in the education division. This was the unit that provided staff education across the institution. At this time Via Health Systems (as it was called) had 10 thousand employees.

During my over 30 years of employment at RGH I had acquired a degree from Michigan State University (via correspondence) in Phycology and Adult Education.

This training came in very handy now that I was educating adults in the workplace. I spent my last seven years at RGH working in HR under a great lady named Nina Morris.

In that position I provided Cultural Diversity Education for 3 thousand employees, and other community organizations and their staff.

I spent 32 years in the lab, and then 7 years in HR at Rochester General Hospital. Twenty-five of those years I spent volunteering for Action for a Better Community Inc., an anti- poverty organization in Rochester, NY.

I am presently in my third marriage and I met all three women at RGH. After I retired from RGH I worked another 5 years for ABC.

I have been affiliated with RGH in some capacity for 55 years. I started working there in 1965, I retired in 2003. Then I served on the RGH Foundation Board for seven years (during the time I was employed at ABC) and for a while when I was retired. Then I came back as greeter & security guard at the Wilson Medical Building for RGHS. This organization is now called the Rochester General Hospital System.

Since I have been with RGHS in some form all of my adult life it is not a strange thing that I met all three of my wives at this facility. Now I finally got it right, and I will die in this marriage!

Rochester General Hospital was called by community people, and many of the employees, "The Plantation." It was called this because of the way people of color were treated at this facility.

The nurses were terrible when it came to patient care for people of color.The security officers were terrible when it came to the way people of color were treated. The doctors were not the best when it came to taking care of people of color and the poor in the Rochester community.

I feel as though I have earned the right to tell the truth about this organization because I have so much of my life invested in it. I have always wanted RGH to do well, and to be respected by this community.

RGH has been serving this community for such a long time that it should have the respect from the people it serves. It does not, and it is not the people of this community's fault.

The patients of color have had all kinds of complaints about how they were treated at RGH. I started working at RGH in 1965, and I must say it was quite bad.

It should be kept in mind that RGH is in the Northeast quandrant of the city of Rochester. The Northeast quandrant of Rochester is the most poverty stricken section of the city. This is where a large segment of the people of color live.

When people of color in that quandrant have an emergency they usually go there, and usually received treatment that no American should have to endure.

The employees of color were targeted by the security team. There were misunderstandings between the security team and employees of color all the time. Many times I was a victim of unfair treatment from the security team. Trust me folks it was bad!

There was this young Black man who was in the process of being hired by the hospital to work in the cafeteria, and he was going through the orientation.

At each orientation the security team would make a presentation on what they did for the institution.

This young man asked a question about the radio security carried with them. I am assuming that he might have had aspirations about becoming an officer. The security officer reported that he had asked this question. That young man was not hired, and was asked to leave the property. In those days there were no officers of color on the team, and none was wanted!

Today there are several officers of color on the security team. They all have radios, and some of them drive security cars. I am now a member of the security team and proud of it. Things have really changed around this place over the years. But that is the way it was then! It is a lot better now, but still not as good as it should be.

Eventually the hospital hired Don DeFrees and put him in charge of the departments that employed most of the people of color. Don quickly learned of the difficulties his staff was having and he instituted the change process. He did not have a choice. He had to start fixing things!

I always say that Don DeFrees was the best thing that ever happened to the Rochester General Hospital System.

When he came on board at RGH he made a concerted effort to get to know the people that worked for him, and the people he would be working with.

We used to have dinners every Friday. His staff and others would bring food in and we would just eat, talk and get to know Don DeFrees.

In those settings he would hear the problems his staff was having with the nurses on the floors, and the security team.

———

He convinced me that he understood and was going to do something about it. Over time he made a difference, but it was not easy for him because wrong had been done for so long that people thought it was right.

When the president of the hospital started the Cultural Diversity Committee to look into setting up a process of education for the staff Mr. DeFrees was there and gave it a good start.

Mr. DeFrees, Easter Tucker, and Lou Parris asked me to join and eventually made me committee chair. These are the people who encouraged me to get out of the lab and start working on this educational process. I am grateful to them all, because this effort changed my life, and started me in a new direction.

It was unlawful for staff to smoke in the restrooms or locker rooms. After lunch some of us would sneak into the locker room and have a smoke.

One day we were smoking in the locker room and Don DeFrees walked in on us. I knew I was wrong! I followed Don into his office and apologized to him for smoking in the locker room. I had to because Don had done all he could to develop a good working relationship with us. I also promised him that he would never catch me smoking in the locker room again. I never did it again!

I am sure there are many stories that would support the claim I am making, but let me share just a few that happened to me.

I was working one weekend at the lab. We would have to feed all of the animals, let the dogs out and clean their cages. This was hard and dirty work! On the weekend we would park near the lab in an area designated no parking. We knew we were not supposed to park there, but it was the weekend, and no traffic was coming through. "Four hours on Saturday and Sunday would not hurt anything," we always said.

On this particular day I had completed my work and I was taking a shower. The security had made good use of the minority law and had hired a couple of White females. There were no Black security guards at that time.

This young lady security guard came into the lab, came into the bathroom where I was taking a shower, and told me I had to move my car right this minute. I drew the curtain back and said, "Right now!?" She turned red as an apple and ran out of the bathroom. She also wrote me a ticket. This ticket was one of the many I had received.

Now I must admit that all of this was not the fault of the security team. The employees of color did fight back the best way we could by doing things that would bring out the worst in the security officers. After all I was parked illegally. But she should have never walk into the bathroom knowing I was in there. I know she heard the shower going!

It was just crazy! Lord forgive me!

Then there was this day I was going home. I was following the access road from the rear of the property to Portland Ave. One of the female security guards had stopped and was giving directions to a customer. She was headed one way and the customer was heading in the other. I stopped behind the security car for a minute to wait for them to finish. They kept talking, so I decided to go between the two cars and continue on my way.

After I passed through the security car came rushing up behind me with the emergency lights flashing and cut me off at one of the turns. She was angry because I had went between the two cars. She felt that I should have waited.

She jumped out of the security car and stood in front of my car. I could not go anywhere because she had the road blocked off!

She yelled at me and said you better not move this vehicle! Then she took out her night stick (security does not carry them anymore), and hit the hood of my car as hard as she could. She put a dent in the center of the hood about the size of a dime.

My friends you have to understand that this was a brand new 1979 Chrysler New Yorker that I had just bought. I had only made a few payments on it by this time! It was the first big car I ever owned.

When she hit my car I went BLANK. All I could see was RED. This was bad (Don DeFrees loves to hear me tell this story). I lost my MIND!

I took my time and went to the trunk of my car and retrieved this big stick I kept for people who disagreed with me.

I took the stick out, took my time and walked back to the open driver's door. I leaned over it and extended that stick in her face. I told her that if she hit my car again I was going to whip her ass with that stick. I meant it when I said it, but immediately I wished I had not said it!

She just stood there with her hands on her hips and said nothing. I am sure she was regretting hitting my car, as I was regretting what I had just said. I sat down in the driver seat and started to pray. "God please don't let her hit my car again because if she does I will have to do what I said. Please God!" By this time I had come back from wherever I had been the last 20 seconds or so.

This was a bad place to be, my friends. I was mad and scared! In my mind I could see myselkf in the back of a police car, handcuffed and on my way to Attica for hurting that White girl.

She did not hit my car again. I requested she call another officer because I was not going to talk to her any further. The matter was settled without further incidence. Praise the Lord!

I still have that stick as a reminder of how my life could have changed in an instant. I never got the hood repaired, and I had that car for ten years. That dent stayed there as a reminder to me. That was one of the worst few moments in my life. It could have gone to a bad place. Thank you Lord!

When I was doing the cultural diversity education for the hospital complaints pertaining to diversity came to my office. I had staff and patients telling me how they were mistreated at RGH.

The ED (Emergency Department) was the worst place because most of the people who came in for an emergency situation received unwarranted treatment. Many left for home more hurt and angry than when they had come in.

I did not want the place where I worked to continue on this track. I wanted things to get better.

Many of the people who experienced the cultural diversity training said it made a difference. Many said they did not want any part of it and did not participate.

I still get compliments on the training, so I feel it was worthwhile. It is now 2013 and this institution, like many others in Rochester, NY, would benefit from this kind of education.

Diversity education should be an ongoing process if you want your organization to be successful in the 21st century.

Birthday Parties at 51 Spiegel Park

During the years of my employment at RGH I got to know many people who were born in the month of August. Some of us decided that we would have an annual "Pig Roast" in the month of August.

At the time I was living with my sister and best friend *"Cat."*

I had remodeled the basement. I had a sitting room and a bedroom with the bed hanging from the ceiling. This was my bachelor pad.

There were 8 years between my first marriage and my second marriage. Those 8 years I lived with my sister *"Cat"* in the basement.

That was the time I got dampness in my shoulders. It has persisted until today. Every now and then I can still feel it.

These were also the years I was busy doing AMWAY. Man, I sold enough Amway products to buy me a new car.

Those were some great years. This was the time I found out what it felt like to be debt free.

Those parties where something else. Cat had an enormous yard. We would dig a whole to roast the pig, invite all of our friends and party all night.

Freddie Perry was born on Aug 3rd, I was born Aug 6th, George Miller was born Aug 10th. We had somebody born on every day in the month of August. Everybody would pitch in and help out with the food, the booze, and the cooking. Freddie Perry and I would roast the pig. Party all the time, party all the time!

We had our lodge brothers from Buffalo and Niagara Falls come to the party.

My friend Ozzie Rambow was the DJ. What a mess that was.

This was a time in my life when I was running wild. I was no longer under the strong hand of my father. I was no longer restrained by the rules of marriage. I was doing Amway which meant I was meeting new people all the time. I was doing everything I thought I could do, and the easy ones I was doing two times.

I needed some discipline in my life and I knew it. I had a heart to heart conversation with my big sister Allene. She suggested I join the Masons. She felt that it would provide me with the discipline I was seeking.

It did, and I have been involved ever since.

So when we had those great parties we would invite the Masonic brothers from Rochester, Buffalo, Syracuse, and Niagara Falls.

We would prepare flyers and spread them all over Rochester, and when a person attended one, they would surely be back next year. Each year it got bigger and bigger!

That yard at my sister's house could accommodate a couple of hundred people. There was a large flat concrete slab in the middle of the yard to dance on, and the party was on.

We would alert the neighbors so no one would call the police. Some of the neighbors attended also, and all of the people on the street would come.

The music was loud, the food was good, and the people at work would be talking about that party for months.

There was no need for anyone to spend a lot of money hosting a party.

If you have twenty friends that will cook and bring food, some people who don't mind spending a little money ($15.00) and help to do some work, you could have a massive party, and lots of fun.

That's what we did every year for several years of "The August Birthday Pig Roast".

I can think of at least three couples that are now married that met at those parties. It was in the middle of the summer and everyone who heard about it came to have some summer fun.

I don't ever remember any fights taking place. There were a few people there with people they were not supposed to be there with though! Oh Well!

Nowadays, in the 21st Century, everybody wants to know how much the other person is spending? How could I come to a party and not spend anything?

Nobody thinks about the group anymore. People just think about what is in it for I, me, and mine? So sad!

This was an event we planned for all summer. Most of the people involved in the planning worked at RGH and/or lived in Rochester.

In Rochester, NY we have nine months of winter, and three months of summer, maybe. That gave us plenty of time to plan a great outing in August.

Everyone knew where it was going to be, that never changed. Everyone knew what they had to do because we did it every year. The plan was just to get more people to come the next year, and that happened every year.

After the party was over late at night (or early in the morning) we had to make sure all of the food that was left over left when the people left. We did not have any extra space to store food so we had people carting plates back to Buffalo and everywhere.

When people left those parties they would eat for three days back home. It was really great!

We all worked together to make this happen, and it did not cost anybody much money.

The Beach House in Charlotte

During those years between my first and second marriage I applied for a job at the Beach House on Beach Avenue out in Charlotte, New York.

A club of wealthy businessmen owned a beautiful beach house that they used for their meetings and lavish parties.

I will always believe that I was hired for this job because I am a Mason. When I went in for the interview I met this tall, red-headed White man who looked at my Masonic ring throughout the entire interview.

He asked me some questions, and I know I answered them correctly, because I know my stuff! Thanks to Daddy Melvin!

I was informed that they usually hired a man and woman team (or husband and wife) so that the woman could assist in the kitchen. I assured him that I would provide assistance to the cook. Plus the cook did not want anybody in her kitchen but her. She was a great cook too!

The cook was a little old White lady and we hit it off really well. She would ask me to take out the garbage after the parties, and sometimes ask me to lift something for her. Beyond that she prepared those great meals all by herself. She always left me plenty in the frig.

The tall red-headed man told me in the interview that this was the first time in twenty years they would hire a single man to be out there around their wives. I know me being a Mason helped!

There were many times the wives would have lunch parties and only women would be on the property. I would plan my time to avoid those parties. I did not want the husbands to worry about their wives and this Black man being on the property at the same time.

I would make sure the pool was clean, and the yard was clean and cut.

There were two large ball rooms, several setting rooms with fireplaces, large TVs, a lavish kitchen, and a 50 thousand gallon pool in the backyard. You could throw a rock from the side of the pool and it would land in Lake Ontario. This place was magnificent!

My live-in quarters was a two bedroom apartment upstairs over the kitchen. It was very nice.

There was room enough for 30 cars to park in the front, and the Lakeshore Golf Course was across the street. I used to find golf balls in the parking lot and throw them across the street on the course. I was not playing golf at that time in my life! What a pity!

They were looking for someone to take care of small repairs: cut the grass, trim the hedges, clean the pool, etc. You had to live there so you would be assessable to them when they were there (rent free).

There was no pay other than **rent free**! This of course was plenty for me. I was still working at the hospital full time, and this was part time work!

They only used the place from Memorial Day through Labor Day. The rest of the year the pool was covered, and there was very little grass to cut between September and May. The place was "ALL MINE."

Part of my responsibility was to live there the months they were closed, and make sure everything was ready for opening in May. You know I loved this job!

My friend Lee Hendricks told me that he could not have me living in a place like that without a good reel and rod so he bought me one.

I would go out in the yard and dig up a few worms, bait a hook, go to the edge of the lake in the evening, and catch my dinner. Then I would go into that lavish kitchen and bake or fry my dinner. I had friends to come out and visit. I had friends spend the weekend or the week. The place was mine!

The owners would leave lots of food in the freezer and storage cabinets, and wine and liquor. Everything a man needed! I was told that when they were away during the winter months the place was mine. You would have to see this place to understand! God is good!

They had a wonderful lady that prepared meals for them when they had their meetings. The wives would have lunch gatherings and swim in the pool. All this would go on while I was at work, or in the city having fun. The cook would always leave me something to eat because I provided her with whatever assistance she needed.

They had an account with the hardware store on Lake Ave so I could get whatever I needed to do repairs to the place. I could go up to the paint store and get paint on their account to keep the place looking great. They loved me and I loved working there.

It was a great three year experience (1985-1988).

One year the NYS Grand Lodge had their meeting in Rochester, New York.

I decided to throw a party at the Beach House with about 50 Brothers and Sisters from all over NYS.

It was during the winter and the view of the lake the night of the party was magnificent. After all of the meetings were completed at the downtown hotel I invited a special group of Masons and Eastern Stars out to the beach house for a party.

During the day at lunchtime some of us had made a dry-run so everyone would be able to find the place. We stopped by a store and purchased what supplies we needed and it was party all the time; party all night long.

Some of the guys from RGH would come out after work and we would put something on the grill and take a dip in the pool. I had to play host and make the girls feel welcome. We would lie around on the floor in sleeping bags in front of the fireplace sipping on wine. It was great!

Many days I would take Daddy Melvin and Mrs. Pearl out to the lake in the morning so they could fish all day. They could dig up some worms out of the flower gardens and go in the back of the beach house and fish in the lake. After work I would take them home in the city. I would leave the back door open so they could go in the house and rest, and them go back and fish some more.

Mrs. Pearl would go in the sitting room and watch her "stories" (Soap operas) while Daddy Melvin fished. It was great! The place was mine. I would let the White club members know these were my relatives so they would not call the police!

There were no Black people living on Beach Avenue that I was aware of. I was the only one, and I was living on the job.

I would get up early in the morning to go to work at RGH, and it would be late at night when I came home. The only time people saw me was when I was cutting the grass, or cleaning out the pool.

After Labor Day the neighbors would start leaving for all parts South and West for the winter. Then the place would be all mine. The times I had in that place!

Sometimes in Rochester we would have great weather well into October, and I would make good use of those days.

The club members lived in Rochester but they would have their parties and club meeting at the beach house. The rest of the time the place was not in use except by me!

After a while a wealthy remodeling company owner bought the place, remodeled it and moved his family there. I have only seen the place a couple of times since I moved out, and then only from the outside. I would assume the place is done up well inside. It was already beautiful.

The new owner informed me that I had two months to find another residence as after that the construction and remodeling would begin.

He seemed to be a very nice man and it was a pleasure to know him. He told me that he was planning to put $15,000 worth of drywall to create rooms and changes for him and his family.

I thank God for those three years. I moved back in with my sister *"Cat."* I had never moved all of my belongings out of *Cat's* house so ending this great experience was simple.

Chapter Six

My Years at Action for a Better Community Inc.

I was working at Rochester General Hospital from 7am in the morning until about 4pm in the early afternoon. After this I would go home and do nothing ie play music, eat, watch TV, and then go to bed. This was not a lifestyle that I liked, or wanted.

I needed to find something to do with my spare time. I had a friend who worked for Action for a Better Community Inc. It was suggested that I volunteer at ABC. I agreed. I figured I could always quit if I did not like it.

I started volunteering for ABC in 1977. When I found out what I would be doing, and meeting Mr. James "MAMBA" McCuller (the Executive Director at that time) I was ready to go!

I began working with the Steering Committee at ABC. This committee served as the eyes and ears of the community. The group reported to ABC what the low income people of the Rochester area and surrounding areas needed, and wanted.

I did this for twenty five years and then moved on to the Board of Directors. I served as president of the board of directors for seven years. I got to know the agency very well, and became friends and/or associates with most of the staff.

When I was sitting on the ABC Steering Committee we were always engaged in activities that got us close to the people. This closeness gave the agency the inside track as to the things the community people needed, and wanted.

The Steering Committee would try to educate the community residents on the importance of voting, and getting involved in the things that impacted them the most.

The Steering Committee assisted other organizations in providing the basic needs of the people. This committee held food drives at churches, sponsored afterschool programs for the children, and helped incarcerated individuals stay connected with their families.

The Steering Committee started a program called the ABC Prison Workforce.

The Prison Workforce group is composed of people who want to maintain their connection to family members incarcerated in the local jails and state prisons.

This program grew to where we were spending weekends in prisons and jails working with the inmates providing all kinds of assistance. We even got connected to inmate families and ABC could provide the services we were known for. This program just grew in all directions.

If you were to calculate the time I spent working with inmates in prison, you could say I spent a year in prison. We were in the Attica Correctional Facility all day on Saturdays, and Wednesday evenings in Groveland Correctional Facility.

The education for HIV & AIDS grew out of this work. The drug and rehab assistance that ABC provided had its roots in some of the work this program had done. It was a perfect connection to ABC over all.

The process was that some of the members of the steering committee also sat on the ABC Board of Directors. This completed the connection of the people on the streets to the decision makers of the organization, and assisted in the development of programs and how the agency served the people.

My experience working at the RGH and my experience in the field of patient care and health care helped the leadership of ABC to put me where they could use me best.

James McCuller saw my interest in health care and, knowing that I was working for RGH, asked me to follow the development of HIV/AIDS as it became big news in the early 1980s. As a result I learned a lot about the disease. When the position for Director of the Action Front Center became open, I applied.

The work I was doing at RGH at that time was running out. I was just about at the end of my career for RGH with 30 plus years of employment.

I loved volunteering at ABC, and I thought it might be fun to work there. Working at the HIV center would be something that I was familiar with, so I applied, and was interviewed.

They chose someone else for the job, but my friend and CEO of ABC found out that I was looking for other employment. He made me one of his deputies. This was one of the best things that ever happened to me! I started doing something I had come to love, and was getting paid more than I had ever thought possible.

So I retired from RGH after 40 years, and worked for ABC for 5 years. I loved every minute of it.

As Deputy Director of Community Services Division I was the manager of five programs:

-Action Front Center: HIV/AIDS Intervention & Education.
-Community Building in Action: Grassroots Community Building & Development.
-New Directions: Drug & Alcohol Rehab Assistance.
-Ontario County CAPP: Community Assistance & Community Building.

-Home Weatherization & Home Ownership Program.

The program directors of each of these groups were very good at what they did and they trained me on the responsibilities of these programs.

I was familiar with what they did from a board member perspective, but learning the day to day activities was a new experience. All the staff was very helpful in me learning my new job.

As I volunteered at ABC the Director (James McCuller) started the Black Men Study Group. This was a group of African American Men who came together on a weekly basis to study Black history.

We read books and talked about what we had read. We had discussion sessions on any subject one of the members wanted to talk about. Mamba (James McCuller) forced us to talk about ourselves, our jobs, our families, and as a result we bonded in ways men rarely do. Some of us became lifelong friends as a result of that group.

The group was founded by James "Mamba" McCuller in 1989, and James died suddenly in 1992. We did our best to keep the group going.

We called the group OMAD: "Organization for Men of African Descent." We became known in the community as James McCuller's "baby Mambas." We were meeting and doing well. We sponsored a weekend conference and brought in a guest speaker from Washington D.C.

We received some money from a local church group to start a women's group. When we got the money the dissention started as to how to spend the money and the group fell apart.

The friendships that were developed have remained strong until this day.

When James Norman became CEO of ABC I was serving on the board of directors. Soon after James Norman came onboard I started working with him and learning how to be board president.

After a few years he asked me to come onboard as staff.

The transition from volunteer to staff came easy because I had been working with the agency and its people for so long.

As part of my job in community action I was to plan, and implement the African American Community Health Fair.

This provided me with the opportunity to work with community health providers (like RGH), and other hospitals. This also provided me with the opportunity to work with drug companies, and other community service organizations.

This job also provided me the opportunity to work with and get to know many of the pastors of churches in our community. This was a very large community event that took place on an annual basis. I enjoyed this experience very much.

Now that James Norman was at the head of the agency we started to see some major changes. The voting process to identify steering committee members was changed. That process got a lot of community involvement but it cost the agency 20 thousand dollars every two years.

The Community Health Fair was costing 20 thousand dollars every year. ABC paid about 7 thousand dollars of that. We (my committee) had to raise the rest!

One of the things James Norman was asked to do as the new CEO was to cut cost and save the agency money wherever he could.

These two events were costly, and had to be changed. Mr. Norman believed in process, and all those processes changed, and the agency was off and running.

I wish I could take credit for the many things I learned about community action, but I can't. From the day I started volunteering for ABC I was exposed to some of the best people in this field. I was allowed to study with them, learn from them, and watch them do their thing. I loved it so much!

When I became staff at ABC I felt that I would be working there the rest of my life. But RGH had taken too much out of me and I got tired very quickly. I did not want to retire, but I was getting tired, and just could not hang. I was 62 years old after 5 years at ABC as staff, and I was surprised how tired I was.

I thought about my responsibilities at ABC all the time. When I got off work on Friday evenings from ABC sometimes it would be midnight before I could clear my mind of ABC stuff.

If there was nothing going on that Saturday (and many Saturdays there were) I could clear my mind until Sunday afternoon, but then I would start thinking about ABC stuff again. James tried to help me with this issue, but I wanted to do everything, and soon learned I could not.

My time at ABC, working with James McCuller and James Norman, was like going to college. I learned so much from these two men, and they put me in places where I could learn. I am so grateful to those two, and the staff of ABC.

I am also amazed at how similar the two of them were. They both were very good golfers, they both were well read on many subjects, and they both were excellent teachers.

They both were great leaders of an agency that has been so much a part of my life here in Rochester, New York.

Chapter Seven

Marriages of the Man

First Marriage

I started working at Rochester General Hospital as soon as I arrived in Rochester NY. As earlier stated I worked one year at West Side Division. The lab moved to RGH North Side Division in Jan. 1966. I met my first wife in Feb. 1966.

She was working in the dietary department at RGH, she was 17 years old, and I was nineteen years old. She had one little baby, and he was one month old.

I was friends with her mother before I ever met her, because we both worked at the Westside Division together.

Her mother and I were part of the group of employees that moved over to the North Side Division. I think that knowing her mother helped in the development of the relationship because her mother knew what kind of person I was, and something about me.

We became friends, and starting dating right away. We spent time together until June 1966 when I was drafted into the US Army. The two years I was away in the Army, I received a letter from her every other day, and after I returned home we got married in September 1968.

Once we were sure that this was what we both wanted we went to the court house and got married. We were too young, and we had no money for a wedding!

The thing that made our relationship click was the partying we did.

In those days the "elite" of RGH had a party every two weeks when we were paid.

The party would move from house to house every two weeks. The ladies would bring food and the men brought the drinks. I loved to have fun, and she did too!

When we arrived at the party she would go her way to have fun with friends, and I would go my way and party with other friends.

We may not have seen each other throughout the party but everyone who knew us knew who she was going home with. We knew how to have a good time.

Like me, my first wife got along with most people well. We made friends easily, and loved to have fun. We would have people over all the time for dinners and parties.

It was work (sometimes two jobs) and school for the both of us all the time.

After we were married I adopted the son she had and gave him my father's name, Caldwell. Now there were three people for whom I was responsible.

We were both very young, loved to party and have a good time. We were both working and going to school at the same time. People used to say they could not understand how we kept having babies because we were rarely together.

My wife at that time worked mostly nights, and I worked days. Most times we did not need a babysitter for the children. Of course Daddy Melvin and Mrs. Pearl were a big help!

We had a total of four children: two boys and two girls.

We were so busy working and raising children that the time went by very quickly.

My first car was a 1968 Ford Mustang 2+2. When I wasn't driving it my wife was always gone somewhere with it. We were always on the move!

When the Ford Pinto first came out we bought two. My wife drove one and I drove the other.

As we grew apart times got bad, and the marriage was over. We broke up (separated) and went back together several times before we called it quits. Altogether we were marriage for 12 years.

At that time it was popular to divorce yourself. You could do all of the running around collecting the required documents, and take that information to the divorce office. They would then arrange the documents, do all of the typing, and get the papers ready to be submitted. The process went smoothly, you paid the money, and you and the other person became exes.

During our marriage I had to go through her long hospital stay from open heart surgery. Seeing her that way was something I had a hard time dealing with. We saw the whole thing through though.

Having love ones go through a major illness is something that stays with you. Thank God we are all still here to talk, and I can write about it.

I worked in the hospital setting for a long time. I still have problems being around sick people. It is just so painful for me. I think I feel their pain, and I just can't stand it...

The two of us have remained friends over the years and we have worked together to raise our children.

They are all adults now and are parents themselves.

I contributed to the demise of our relationship and will never cast blame. My mother used to say, "It takes two to tango! Very rarely can one person make a marriage, or break one up alone. It takes two!"

It is okay to party when you are young, but sooner or later you are going to have to grow up and start building a life. If you wait until you are 35 you are on the borderline of failure. If you wait until you are 40, it is too late.

Too many people never grow older than thirty-five and live their lives there. This is not a good thing when you have children coming up behind you!

Second Marriage

Eight years passed between my first and second marriage. It was a difficult time for me because I was so used to being married.

My work at RGH and volunteering at ABC kept me busy. I got involved with Amway during that time and that kept me moving, and making a little money.

Then I met my second wife. She also worked at RGH. I was divorced from my first marriage, and she was divorced from her first marriage also.

We became friends, and over time we starting dating.

In 1988 we were married and started our life together (although we had known each other for a long time). This was a new experience for both of us. We had both worked at the hospital for many years and had known each other very well. We both retired from RGH.

I always liked going to work early so I could get my coffee and relax before I started work. This was also a habit of hers so many mornings we would have our coffee together in "The Red Lion."

This may very well have been the process how we got to know each other beyond just being friends.

My second wife and I were married for 15 years. I assisted her in raising her children. She had three girls and two boys. Over the years we became very close as a family.

During the years of my second marriage I built relationships with those children that have helped to make me who I am today.

I like to think that I never interfered with their relationship with their biological father. I believe that all involved should work together for the sake of the children.

The children from my second marriage got along well with the children from my first marriage. The girls got along very well.

My mentor James McCuller told me that the problem for my second marriage would be the children from the first. This was not the case for me because the children got along very well.

The thing that made this second relationship click was her "cool and calm" in times of difficulty. I could take issues to her and she would help me work through them.

We had fun together when no one else was there, and no one else needed to be there! I feel that being friends first is an asset to any marriage.

I like to think that people should wait until they know who they are before they try to become one with someone else.

I tell young people to take their time in making the big decision of getting married. I tell them to become friends first. That way you can always be best friends even if the marriage doesn't work.

My second wife was not one for a lot of partying and going out all the time. We had fun just the two of us.

She was one for being on time. I liked that because I liked to be on time for events we attended.

During this time in my life I was involved in my work at RGH, and in my volunteering at ABC. I took my wife on several business trips to conferences for both RGH and ABC. These trips provided her with an opportunity to get away from the children, and the house.

My second wife was very close to my sister Betty. They were very good friends.

My second wife is from Trinidad and I visited there two times during our marriage. The first time was after we were married so that I could meet her family. The second visit was after her mother died.

Because we all live in the same city we see each other frequently in passing. I have always worked to maintain friendships because good ones are so hard to find. Also, we were very good friends long before we became married.

I have always loved to cook and "bump" around in the kitchen. She was a good cook but did not like doing it. This worked out very well for both of us.

Good food was a big thing for both of us and she allowed me to work the in kitchen like I wanted. We both enjoyed making the two cuisines work together.

In those days I ate food just because it was there! During my second marriage I became as heavy as I had ever been (255lbs).

We had agreed from the beginning of the marriage that I would not get involved in the rearing of her children to the point where any of them would ever have to remind me that I was not their father. I worked very hard to make sure that that never happened.

We agreed from the beginning that we would never fight over money. I hate those kinds of arguments because they can get ugly quickly. People tend to say things they later regret when you fight over money. I don't ever remember us arguing about money. That is sure not because we had so much, because we did not!

As in many marriages we just started to grow apart.

During this relationship (long before we were married) I saw her go through a major illness of sorts.

She has a set of twins from her first marriage. Those girls almost caused their mother's death.

We were just friends during those days but I went to the hospital to visit her and observed her in a very bad state. Again, I thank God that we are all still here to talk, and I can write about those days.

Mothers have always put their children first, and that is a good thing, sometimes. But you can never put your children before your husband.

One reason: the children will grow up and go away. Once this happens you and your husband can grow old together.

When you start to say "No" to your children they will "kick you to the curb," and say you are a bad person.

The second reason: God never told you to cleave unto your children and become one with your children. But you are told to cleave unto your husband/wife, and become one with your spouse. Of course that goes for the man too!

I did not say put your man before your children, I said put your husband before your children.

Chapter Eight

This time I have it Right!

Eventually I met my present wife, Peggy, and would you believe she also worked at RGH! You have to remember I have worked at RGH for 40 years. Most of the people I know I met while working at RGH, or volunteering for ABC.

There was a place we called "The Red Lion" at RGH. "The Red Lion" was the breakroom in the basement of the hospital where the "elite" took their breaks.

We would have coffee in the morning, our morning break, lunch, and our afternoon break in "The Red Lion." Some of the staff met there on their way out to connect with their rides home.

We had our meals in "The Red Lion" and played cards there during our breaks. This space was the center of activity for the RGH elite.

Before Peggy and I got to know one another very well I would see her in the halls of the hospital. She would be on her way to a meeting of some kind and I would be moving about through the hospital also.

I would always say "Hi," and say something funny. That's just the way I am. She had the prettiest smile! She would always be dressed so neatly.

I first met my present wife when a group of us began meeting in the cafeteria for breakfast. Peggy decided to join this group.

You know how stuff gets started in the workplace: people are seen together a couple of times, and the rumor mill starts.

The next thing I knew the word was all over the place about Peggy and I, ...and nothing was going on ....at that time. We were just developing a friendship.

There are certain professions where women outnumber men by large margins. Social work and health care are two of them.

At RGH women were about 85% of the working population. Most of my friends were at work. In a hospital setting it is never strange for a male to have lots of female friends.

A few years passed and my second marriage had "hit the rocks." Peggy's marriage had gotten to the point where she actually moved away for a while. Eventually she returned to Rochester.

When Peggy did return to Rochester (and had been back in town for a while) we saw each other and began to renew our friendship.

The thing that made it click for us was her humor.

Peggy could tell stories about her family and her life that made me laugh. Those who know me know I love to laugh. She could do that so well.

She is also quite the speaker, and speaking is something I love to do also. Peggy has never been afraid to speak in front of a group of people.

I admire anyone who can stand in front of a group of people and be themselves. Peggy can hear a person talk for about five minutes, and then she can sound just like them. This is her gift. I hope you get a chance to hear her use it.

Sometimes when I go to work and come home she has developed another one of my friends and sounds just like them. It is really funny!

In getting to know Peggy I also got to know some of the members of her family. One relative in particular I came to know was her Aunt Belle.

The first time we went over to meet Aunt Belle I fell in love with her, and we became the best of friends.

Aunt Belle was one of the most praying people I ever knew. You would love to hear this woman pray. I believe that God loved to hear this woman pray!

We use to have prayer meetings at our house and we would take turns praying, and everyone would love for Aunt Belle to pray. Then we would eat and just get to know one another.

Aunt Belle became one of those women I adopted as my mother. There have been several in my life!

As was stated earlier I lost my mother at a very early age. When I would meet an older woman and our spirits clicked, she would become my mother.

Aunt Belle nursed the relationship between Peggy and I. I love my Aunt Belle! I also came to call Aunt Belle's daughter my sister. We still call each other sister and brother.

In 2003 Peggy and I were married and there were other special people added to my list. Peggy has three children: one boy and two girls.

Once we decided to get married we started planning our wedding. I had never had a wedding before so this would be something new for me. My previous marriages had been at the Justice of the Peace's office.

Of course every marriage is a book in itself. But this book is not just about marriage, this is about Freddie the man, and how do you as the reader get to know him better.

I was fearful about our age difference at first but she helped me to get over that. She is 13 years my junior, and she is so much fun to be around.

I think the age thing was a problem for me because my father used to say, "Stay in your class boy! Stay in your class!" At first I thought I was working outside of my class because of our age differences.

I have always been one to think that loving someone should be easy, and not complicated. I never liked the idea that you have to work hard to make a relationship work.

If you love the person, and the person loves you back, then it should work. It should be easy!

I think you should take people as they are, and allow them to become whatever they are capable of becoming. Then you both can go through the process together. In a marriage when two people work to become one neither of them are ever the same again.

At the wedding there were 150 attendees. We decided to have two preachers marry us: my brother (who is a minister), and my pastor, Rev. Cherry.

This was a Masonic wedding and all of my brothers and sisters took part in it. It was something to see!

With so many witnesses I am committed to seeing this marriage through. Also, I am too old to do anything else!

I must like being married because I have always been in one (except for a few years between marriages one and two)!

We have been married for 10 years, and we have a home we both like. We live in a neighborhood we both like, and we both have people in our lives that we like.

I tend to hang with people from the place where I work, and the community people I have worked with to make changes for the better.

Throughout my life I have tended to socialize with the people I worked with, my lodge brothers, some of my church members, and the community people with whom I volunteered.

My wife and I attend different churches, and we have no problem with that. I have always said that where a person worships is a very personal thing. You have to be happy in your church setting, and if you are not; you should move until you find one that makes you happy.

I have only been a member of three churches all my life: Zion Hope MBC in Sanford, St. John MBC in Rochester, and now Aenon MBC in Rochester.

I have always considered myself a down South Bible-toting Baptist!

When we decided to get married I was attending St. John Missionary Baptist Church, and Peggy was attending Zion Hill MBC.

We agreed that we would find a church that neither of us was familiar with and start all over. So we started visiting churches, and decided on Aenon. I fit right in at Aenon because you know I love Sunday school!

It is strange to me how Black women in the community at large (and in churches specifically) treat one another. At Aenon things did not work out well for Peggy. We decided that she would go back to her old church (Zion Hill).

During her time away the pastor of Zion Hill had died and things changed.

When she returned the changes that had taken place were not to her liking so she starting looking for a church home that made her comfortable.

You have to hear her tell you the story of her search process. It is another of her funny, but true, stories.

Peggy has now found a church that she likes, and we will see what happens in the future.

I am happy at Aenon because my involvement is with the Sunday school, and I love the group of people with whom I have come in contact. Additionally, my pastor is a good friend of mine and I like being in his presence, and in that church.

During the early years of this marriage I went through an illness with Peggy that almost took her away from me. Any surgery is major, and we went through one together with a long recovery.

I remember I had to go to work in the morning, come home and get her some lunch, and make sure she was okay at home.

It was a tough time for her and I thank God she is still here and we can talk about it with smiles on our faces. Peggy is up and well again and now I can write about it.

The reason I feel that this marriage is it is because when my friend and mentor James Norman met her he said that we were good for one another.

If it is true that opposites attract we are good for one another. We we are opposites on everything. If I say green, she will say blue!

In the yard at our home she plants flowers, and I plant food. This is something that came with and through my parents. No matter how hard we try we cannot get rid of, or change, the effect of our genes.

We both like to entertain so we are always planning a gathering of some kind. She spends a lot of time keeping the house clean, and ready for company. I like to spend time out in the yard doing things to make the outside look inviting and comfortable for the people that come over to visit.

The most visitors we get are from her family members and a few friends. When I have a large project to do I call on my young lodge brothers to come over and assist. Most of the time they come and help.

I do not get a lot of visits from my family members and I could never understand why. Some families are much closer than others, but we love one another anyway.

We all have little things about us that others dislike. If you love someone, you do not love them in spite of those things: you love them because of those things.

My wife is full of advice about everything, much like my sister Verdene. Sometimes I take her advice and sometimes I don't.

My pastor always reminds me that sometimes you had better listen to your wife because sometimes she is right!

I think that a good way to get to know someone is to know how they think. To know how they feel about issues people talk about, or not talk about.

So I have come up with some issues that people tend to stay away from in conversation, and share my opinion on these issues so you can get to know me better, and know how I think.

Chapter Nine

Getting to know the Man

When I was in the Toastmasters Club I presented this introductory presentation, and it set the tone for my short stay in that club.

This presentation is designed for the members of the club to get to know me. I hope that it serves the same purpose for the readers of this book.

"THINGS THAT MAKE ME ANGRY."

First, I must share with you the difficulty I had in choosing the title of this presentation. I had three choices:

One: "Things that piss me off," which is an American colloquium. Everybody knows what it means but I felt it might offend some, so I chose it not.

Two: "Things that make me mad." When I consulted Mr. Webster & Friends I found that mad means, "Insane; a disordered mind." When one is mad they are completely unrestrained, incapable of being explained or accounted for; furious; frantic, and displaying WILD, chaotic activity."

That is certainly not what I feel when I am confronted with the situations I am about to share. So I chose it not.

Third: "Things that make me angry." Mr. Webster & Friends state that angry means: "wrathful"; (or my favorite) "painfully inflamed." Painfully Inflamed is what I feel when I am confronted with these situations.

So, the title of my presentation is:

"<u>Things that make me angry</u>"!

It makes me angry, or it painfully inflames me when I hear people say there are things that Americans should not discuss.

Things like Capital Punishment (the death penalty), Abortion, and Prayer in the public schools; Sex and Sexuality.

My fellow Toastmasters, America is still a developing country. We have people coming to America from all parts of the world, with their own languages and their own customs. If we are to remain the greatest nation on the planet there should be nothing we cannot talk about, discuss, or debate.

Race, religion, politics, ...what is the problem America? These are the very issues we should be talking about, so that when we send our sons and daughters off to fight in other countries (and at home for America's values) we know, and they know, why they are fighting, and dying.

It painfully inflames me when I hear someone say, "You should speak proper English!" What does that mean in America?

That determination depends on who is judging: someone from London, England, or someone from lower Alabama. With all of the languages and dialects spoken in America it is amazing we communicate as well as we do!

For those of you who feel you speak proper English, go to England.

People tell me that "AINT" is not proper English. Aint is a conjunction for "am not" or "is not." Use in a sentence: "I ain't going to school today,......and anything you say to make me go, it ain't going to work!"

"Proper language" is the words, and combination of words, used in a district, and understood by the people living in that district. These are the things that make it proper.

It painfully inflames me when people say, "I don't see color, I just see people." When I hear that a RED flag goes up that says: "Misinformed Racist."

Children see color. We teach them colors from the time they are born, and when they go to school and mingle with others who look different from them…. they see color. Skin color is the first mode of recognition. Dealing with the issue of color gets in the way a child's primary business: to play.

"You roll me the ball, and I will roll it back. I don't care what color you are! But I do see it!"

Adults see color too! But because we do not have an appropriate language to use in discussing these issues, some say what they think is appropriate, and all it does is inflame the issue.

You insult me when you do not recognize my color. I am not ashamed of my color. On the contrary, I am proud of my color ever since James Brown told me to, "Say It Loud, I'm Black and I Am Proud" in 1968.

You deceive yourself (and me) when you say you don't see my color, big and Black as I am standing up here. Come on America, let's step this thing up a notch!

It painfully inflames me when people say, *"The N- Word."* I don't mean the word Nigger, I mean the phrase, *"N-Word."*

My fellow Toastmasters, the "N-Word" is a phrase that was instituted during the OJ Simpson trial of the early 1990s. It served as a new way for America to say the word "Nigger," without saying the word "Nigger."

America, "Nothing" is an N-Word; "Never" is an N-Word; "No More" is an N-Word.

In 2004 the NAACP had a funeral for the phrase "N-Word." Al Sharpton preached the eulogy, and they put it in a casket and laid it to rest. Now we can discuss the word "Nigger," what it means to you, and what it means to me.

We should really take an in-depth look at what Webster & his friends say about this word!

After this presentation to the Toastmaster's club of predominantly White males my stay was cut to about a year. I never fit in because they knew this was the direction I was going to take!

Opinions of Freddie Lee Caldwell

When I was in the military we used to say, "Opinions are like Assholes: everybody has got one!" These are some of mine.

Again these opinions are designed to help the reader get to know me, what I believe, and how I express those beliefs.

OPINION NUMBER ONE

ABORTION

One of the most controversial subjects in American society today is that of abortion. People are killing other people in the name of saving the unborn children. **In my Opinion** what we need is the answer to two questions: when does life begin; when does life end?

Does life begin at conception, or does it begin at birth?

There are those who believe that life begins when the sperm meets the egg, and the growth process begins. There are those who believe that life begins with the first breath when a child is born.

It would be a shame if we found out later that those doctors who have been killed in the prime of their lives, before they had paid off all those loans, and killed in their living rooms, died for nothing. Many have been found dead in the parking lots of their offices in the name of saving unborn children.

When I was a young man my father told me, "The answer to all of Man's questions is found in the Holy Bible. Throughout my life I have found it to be true.

When Does Life Begin? The Bible says, in Genesis 2:7, "And the Lord God formed man of the dust of the ground, and breathed into his nostrils the breath of life; and man became a living soul."

If the Bible is right the child is being formed while it is in the mother's womb, it is not yet alive! It is being formed.

It does not live until it breathes, and it does not breathe until it is born!

When does life end? The Bible says, in Matthew 27: 50, "Jesus, when he cried again with a loud voice, yielded up the ghost, or spirit."

That means breathe the last breath!

There is a Biblical story of a husband and his wife that were joining the church, and were to sell all they had and give it to the church. You know the story: they held some of the money back, lied about it, and died about it. They gave up the ghost! That means they breathed their last breath!

So there you have **my opinion** on this matter.

Why is it that a woman's immune system is at its weakest point when she is pregnant? It is because her body is fighting a growth that has not always been there. This does not mean that a woman's body is not designed to give birth; however, when she becomes pregnant her body treats the embryo like an invader for much of the pregnancy.

When a child is being developed in the womb there is a membrane that covers the entrance to the lungs. It is there to protect the lungs as they develop. That membrane is broken when the child take its first breathe.

If it is alive before it is born, how does it breathe, for it is submerged in water? It would appear that the breathing has a lot to do with both life and death.

I wonder how many people have considered this point! Many people have died, and many have gone to prison for the rest of their lives. They have been found guilty of taking a life that is living for one that is not yet alive, **in my opinion**.

Opinion Number Two

<u>Women & the Change</u>

In American society the divorce rate is 50% percent. That means half of the people who get married get divorced. There are many reasons why people get divorced, but **In My Opinion**, not enough attention has been paid to women going through the "Change," and the divorce rate.

When a young girl grows into puberty, and begins to have a monthly cycle, a process of about 10 days in duration takes place.

There is a pre-menstrual, menstrual, and post menstrual cycle, each of about three days. During these 10 days the young woman is sometimes totally out of her mind. This is one third of the month, and this time is spent fighting mood swings, and other up and down feelings, all caused by natural hormones. During this time the female body is getting prepared to give birth if the egg is fertilized. If the egg is not fertilized in the time allotted this cycle of cleansing begins. It takes about ten days.

These are lessons that men must learn and understand if they plan to stay married. It appears that about half of them get it!

The other twenty days of the month are fun, and good times. This continues until the woman goes through the "Change" at 40-45 years of age.

The time factor is one/third of the month, one/third of the year, and seven - ten years between the ages of 40 - 55. During these time periods a woman is crazy, and no one knows what is going on, especially the woman.

When she goes through the "Change" she is in this state for thirty days of the month, twelve months of the year, from seven to ten years. This is a time factor of every day, every month, for seven to ten years.

This is usually a time when the children are grown and gone. The children are young adults in high school, or they are away in college. The husband and wife are home alone, and this is the time that men don't understand, and many of them leave under the pressure.

They leave because women going through the "Change" can be so cruel. They know their husband's weak spots, they know what sets him off, and they have no pity.

Men must also understand the woman is not always aware of the hurt and pain she is causing her husband.

They leave because men have feelings too, and they can be hurt. Men must not blame their wives, because the wives are suffering too.

Now for the men: Brothers if you can last through the years of having your lovely wife only 20 days out of the month, and with God's help you can survive the seven to ten years of not having her at all, then you will receive the young lady you married, and have her for the rest of your life. This will be when she is about 55 – 60 years old. Oh, but happy days are here again!

This is a test that only strong men can survive, and education on this issue is required if your marriage is to make it through these years.

I have the utmost respect for those men who have survived those years. You are much more of a man than I.

I could not stay under the pressure of my first marriage, and felt I was educated enough to survive the second wife going through the "Change", but I was not! I plan to stick this one out, and see what the end brings. I am trying marriage for the third time.

So **In my Opinion,** be strong gentlemen, and stick it out. Remember it is not their fault. They are going through the change. This is something that all women must face, and it impacts some differently from others.

You must not go through it with them. You must allow her to go through. You are there for support, and just stand back and let it happen. You can only assist by staying out of the way, and not getting hurt so bad that you leave.

We men are not physically or mentally designed to deal with this, so just try hard to stick it out. If you can, it will be well worth it.

At least this is what the men tell me who have survived!

Opinion Number Three

White People's Job on Blacks & All Americans

At one of our OMAD meetings long ago, Robert Djed Snead posed the question: "Is the job done by White people on Black people completed, or is there more work to be done?"

The "job" means the making of the slave, and people of color hating one's self unto death.

When we think of the job that was done on Blacks in America, we must also think of the educational effort performed on all Americans.

Not only were Blacks taught to be slaves, and to hate one another, all Americans were taught to treat the slaves a certain way. The institution of slavery was meant to last forever. The plan was for it to exist forever, and never change.

Our conclusion was that the job is complete, but a certain amount of maintenance is required every now and then.

In my opinion, the Willie Lynch rule is simple and complete. The rule states that this process would work on any people, in any country, at any time. If this conditioning were applied to any people it would have the same effect that it had on Blacks.

"If you pit the young slave against the old slave.
If you pit the male slave against the female slave.
If you pit the light-skinned slave against the dark-skinned slave.
If you pit the house slave against the field slave.
If you pit the freed slave against the enslaved."

You will all ways have conflict. If you find ways, and create ways, to pit these groups against one another at all levels, all the time, and do it with consistency, for one hundred years, then that people will do it to themselves for the next five hundred years. Mr. Lynch said it could last a thousand years if done properly.

Mr. Lynch taught the Virginia slave masters to work on the woman slave first. Make sure that she understands whatever she needs that she can and must get it from the Master.

The Black female slave was to train the male slave to be strong and dumb. She was to train the female child to do what she has done for her children, and the institution of slavery, would last forever.

If we take the timeline of the 1500s as a starting point, and treat the enslaved African in that manner for one hundred years, until the 1600s, they will do it to themselves for 500 years, we are looking at the year 2100.

My math says we have some 85 more years before most Black Americans will begin to see the light.

Many Black leaders of today see the light at the end of the tunnel, but we are far from the end of the tunnel, and mental freedom.

During the one hundred years that Black Americans were taught to hate one another, the rest of America was being taught how to support this work.

Any White person could approach any Black person and ask questions about who they were, who they belonged to, and where were they going?

Remember: there were no police officers until the slaves were freed. Any White person could ask these questions of any Black person.

The slave had to provide answers or go to jail, or worse!

Just as the hatred for one another is still in effect today for Blacks, Whites still feel that they can inquire of any Black person the same type of information. All Americans are still under the influence of that ancient training.

All Whites were being taught that they were better than Blacks, smarter than Blacks, and everybody was aware of the old adage "If you are White you are all right, if you are Brown you can stick around, but if you are Black, you better step back."

All Americans lived by that rule, and all Americans enforced that rule, even the Blacks.

The way a people is treated in a society, determines how that people will perform in that society. We should see then why Blacks have performed so poorly in the American society.

Opinion Number Four

The Michael Jackson Story

All America watched the story of this young man unfold. We saw him on television as a small child singing and dancing like an adult man with years of musical experience.

We watched his father mold him and his brothers into stars with wealth and fame. Many of us danced to his music, and paid to see him perform. I know I did!

Then we saw the change come, plastic surgery, his hair burned away and the drugs started. Many Americans are still not sure about the little boys, but we do know he never had a childhood, and tried to compensate for that by spending inappropriate time with children.

You have to admit the boy could sing and dance!

Throughout America we see famous people show their good side, and try to hide their bad side. With the media coverage of today they rarely get away with it. He thought America loved him so much that he felt he could do anything, like many others.

It is hard to think that someone who could have such a powerful influence on so many people all over the world could go out that way, but look at Elvis!

He was great at some things and so very bad at others.

Many of the people that were close to MJ warned him about the children, and how he spent time with them. They tried to guide him in how he spent his money, but you can't tell some people anything.

He changed from being Black to being what he thought was White because of his money and his fame. He made some very bad decisions in the people he married, the people he trusted, and the way he lived his life. We all have skeletons in our closets. Those things we have done and don't plan to ever tell anyone!

In my Opinion his life is a great story like many others in the world he lived. The world of entertainment!

I loved most of his music and admired his father for making the Jackson family great. I credit the father more than anyone else.

If it were not for Joe Jackson that family would have lived and died in Gary, Indiana before they all became famous and moved to Hollywood.

I am not surprised at how White people treated him in America. You have to remember that they are as brainwashed as all other Americans when it comes to Black people.

I believe that leaving all the money in the hands of his mother was wrong, but it was his money!

I believe that those washed up brothers of his need to sit down and enjoy their lives; they don't have to work anymore. There were only three people in that family with talent: Joe, Janet, and Michael.

I believe that we should remember the good things that he did for the world, as we remember the few bad things. And if it is all true, they were some bad things!

I also want to remind you that the boy could sing and dance and you know it!

Opinion Number Five

Community Based Organizations & the Church

When I was a child I watched my father worked in the community with and through the churches. I remember people talking about the work he did all over Sanford, Florida.

When I moved to Rochester, New York I started to do similar work in this community. I worked at the Rochester General Hospital for 40 years, and was always involved in things that made it better for my people at work.

In 1975 I was introduced to Action for a Better Community Inc., where I met Mr. James "Mamba" McCuller. ABC is an organization and Mamba was a man dedicated to helping people helped themselves. ABC was the kind of organization I was looking for, and it seemed I was what he (Mamba) and ABC was looking for because the organization was a big part of my life, and I loved every minute of it!

One thing Mamba taught us was, "If you are going to do anything with, or for Black people, you must employ those people sitting in the church on Sunday morning." He referred to them as the "shakers and movers" in any community! I felt this was a true statement because my father worked with all of the churches in my hometown.

I assisted Mamba in getting the community churches to support the work that ABC was doing. We were also taught that before there were organizations like ABC the church was where community people went for assistance in times of trouble.

Right from the start of community action churches and community based organizations have had a very close working relationship in helping people. Churches have always served as a place to reach the community with a newly discovered message.

In my Opinion, over my years of experience working with Pastors and churches, I have found that we have been asking the church to do things it is not charged to do.

I have found that churches are to: preach the Gospel, perform marriages, bury the dead, and maintain the building fund.

ABC and other community based organizations have approached churches for assistance and many times received nothing because this is not what they specialize in, or do very well anymore.

In the 21st Century the church seems to have focused their attention on the money. Many preachers are no longer interested in helping people if there is no money in it. I don't mean money for the church. I mean money for the preacher. It has become a sad affair when we look at how well some of the preachers are living compared to the members of the church.

When the community based organization approaches the church for assistance these days you have to be able to show the church what is in it for them, ...and their pastor. Sad!

The best example I can use is HIV/AIDS.

It took the churches 15 years to understand that they were to help fight this disease. We found that if it was not their charge you were going to have a difficult time getting them to help, especially if it impacted them maintaining that building fund.

We found out about this disease in the early 1980s and had to work the streets with the message of its impact on life, death, and people of color.

By 2000 the church was getting the message, and began to see their role. Community based organizations also began to see their role better as the churches better defined what their community responsibility was going to be into the future.

So, as we approach churches to help solve community problems we must give them a lot of lead time to prepare and to change their focus, or they might not come along. We must be mindful of their charge and ours.

Feeding the hungry, clothing the naked and providing shelter for the shelterless does not always fit into their scope of activities anymore.

Opinion Number Six

HIV/AIDS where did it come from?

At the end of the Second World War, and midway through the Korean War, 16 of the wealthiest families in the world held a meeting. Place unknown.

The purpose of the meeting was to discuss how to extract the wealth from the richest continent on earth: Africa. These families wanted to determine how to identify and lay claim to the gold and diamonds of Africa, and how to make the best use of the riches generated by the oil that was found there.

One of the first concerns was what to do with all of the people on the continent. It was at this time when the designation of First, Second, Third and Fourth World countries came into being. Third and Fourth World countries are very poor with lots of people living in abject poverty. The people of these countries were sick, and dying from all kinds of ailments, and diseases.

The people in these countries had to deal with bad water, bad food, or no food at all. A determination was made to get rid of all of these poor people by assisting them in dying. Accordingly a virus was developed and put into the people of these Third and Fourth World countries (many or most of them in Africa.)

This is the reason why the HIV virus was first discovered in Africa, why it is so potent there, and why it loves Black people who are also poor.

When the HIV virus was found in America all of the efforts to find out where it came from was discouraged.

Instead the emphasis was placed on doing something about it, not finding out where it came from. A story was developed about where it came from but it was almost impossible to verify. The "Monkey story" was told, but the cure was the main thing talked about.

A few years ago when the USA found e-coli in some vegetables it was traced to tomatoes in Florida. The farmers of Florida lost a lot of money because their tomatoes were thought to be infected. The search continued and the source of the e-coli was determined to have come from peppers in Mexico.

The point I am trying to make is that the USA did not stop until it found out where those bad vegetables came from.

Why was not the same effort made to find out where the HIV virus came from? The answer was known by those who developed it, and all efforts to track it down were discouraged.

The people who developed the HIV virus **in my Opinion** were not aware that the wealth of Africa would make those people so mobile, therefore spreading the virus all over the world.

The virus was developed for poor Black people in Fourth World countries, not for traveling businessmen all over the world.

Because the virus got out of the cage, it started to attack everyone who came into contact with it and the world became very concerned. This disease ran rampant for twenty years until it found its focus and now it is honed back in on the original target: poor Black people.

The disease infected all those who were poor, those who were involved in drug use, and those who came into contact with poor infected people.

If you look at the disease and where it is focused as of 2013 you will see who it is infecting the most, and this is true all over the world.

The disease is impacting poor Black people in Haiti, poor Black people in England, poor Black people in the United States, and of course poor Black people in Third and Fourth World countries of Africa.

Opinion Number Seven

Same Sex Marriage

Another one of the most controversial issues in America today is "Same Sex Marriage." First let me say **In My Opinion** there is no such thing. To make it more politically correct we say "same sex marriage."

I am one who believes that the institution of marriage is between a man and a woman.

I am not one who holds anyone responsible for the way they choose to have sex, or who they choose to have it with. This conversation is not about sex. It is about the state of marriage. This is about how we as Americans are going to define that word, and how it will be used in our society.

I have no problems with two people of the same sex living together, nor do I have any problem with two people of the same sex sharing their belongings, and calling their union anything they choose, as long as it is not called "marriage." If you call what two men have "marriage," then what is it that my wife and I have? They are not the same, and can never be the same.

We are all human beings first and, with that said, we owe each other a certain amount of respect.

Why should anyone be judged because of the way they have sex or who they have sex with? Come on America! We have much larger problems to address!

You see until this point I have not used the word "GAY". Please do not refer to the rest of us as "STRAIGHT." To call heterosexual "straight" denotes that homosexual are "not straight." What does that mean? What does "straight" mean?

"GAY," 60 years ago, meant: joyful, colorful, playful, fun loving, and happy. Fifty years ago there was nothing wrong with referring to a man as gay, or saying those peoples are having a gay time. But now this quaint little word has been giving a new meaning. The dictionary, over time, has come to agree with this new definition.

Gay: happily excited, merry; keenly alive and exuberant; having or inducing high spirits; bright, lively; brilliant in color, given to social pleasures. Then (in 1980) a new definition of "gay" was added to the definition. Look up the word "homosexual" in a dictionary today. How did we who speak English allow that happen?

When people ask me my opinion on homosexuality I say, "I don't condemn, and I don't condone!" This means that I don't condemn anyone for choosing this lifestyle, and I don't condone, or agree, that it is the right thing to do.

I am ready to work with, and be friends with, homosexuals but please do not try to convince me that it is the right thing to do. I can't go there! I am also very displeased with the use of the term "gay" in reference to a homosexual. It painfully inflames me!

In any marriage, or civil union, it is the people involved that decide how they live their lives, and who they live them with, plain and simple.

Think about it: when the homosexual marriage is done they refer to one another as wife and wife. How can you have two wives in one marriage? How can you have two husbands in one marriage? I am sorry my friends marriage is the wrong word.

The term marriage has nothing to do with sex. It just does not make sense. I see a union (by whatever name you choose to call it) as a union. A civil union, yes. But a marriage? I cannot honor that!

I also agree, and understand, that we live in a country of laws, and, if we as Americans pass a law that makes it (same sex unions) legal I will respect that law. I will never agree with that law, but I will respect it.

Opinion Number Eight

Pimping from the Pulpit

Down in the neighborhood when we say pimp, we are referring to those who earn their living talking others into working for them, or to keep money flowing in their direction.

Pimping happens when drugs are sold and when clothes are stolen and then sold to community members. There are those who say that the pastor of some churches are pimping the people ie driving luxury cars, dressing in designer suits, and not really working for it.

In this town, like many others across America, pimping from the pulpit is a very good business. If you listen you can hear the pastors of churches talking about the money their church has, and how the "Building Fund" is maintained.

You can hear them brag about the money they (earn), the cars they can buy (or have bought), the clothes they wear, and how much they cost. They talk about how the members scramble to be the preacher's pet.

In my opinion, God is not pleased with the activities that take place in some of the pulpits. The pulpit is supposed to be "Holy Ground" up there.

It is one thing to have a preacher abusing the congregation with lies and trickery, and also having people sitting up there that are known homosexuals. God is not pleased!

Many of the "big" preachers of America now have their wives as ministers also, and getting a salary from the church, ...which is all part of the game. Many of them have other friends and relatives getting into the business, which is all good I suppose.

197

Rev. Bob Harrington of New Orleans, Louisiana says, "Homosexuals should be a part of the church, but not in the pulpit. We should pray for them, not make leaders out of them"!

My big brother is a minister, and he feels that I don't like ministers. This is not true of course. I just call it like I see it.

I feel that ministers are an important part of the community, but many people do not trust them, and with good reason some of the time. But no one can take care of God's business better than God Himself. I am sure in due time He will attend to those preachers who use His name to line their pockets.

One of the things that I dislike is when the money plate is passed, and people put in the plate what they have, or what amount they choose, and then the preacher asks for more. Beg for more; pimp more out of the people.

God loves a cheerful giver. But now the people are being asked for money they don't have, or not willing to give. But the preacher embarrasses them into giving a little more, and this money given unwillingly does no good for the church, or the giver.

That money will not do the pimp (the preacher) any good either, but he feels that he has done his job.

I love God, and I love the church. I do truly love my pastor, because he is my friend too, but all of them need to evaluate where they are, and what they are doing to a poor and unsuspecting people looking at them, and listening to them.

Opinion Number Nine

<u>When to Teach Children about Sex</u>

One of the most talked about subjects in America today is when to talk to children about Sex? I think we all agree that they do need to be taught, but when?

We may agree that the parent should do that. But what about those parents who are afraid, or don't know how to approach this subject with their children?

In my Opinion, it is the school's job to educate the children. They teach our children all the other subjects, why not sex? They learn anatomy, and physiology in health classes at school. The school teaches music, and math; why not sex?

It may well be the responsibility of the parent to follow up on what their children are being taught on some subjects, and parents should support what is being taught, or not. They should not have the right to say what other people's children are being taught, if it is approved by the school board.

This would take care of those parents who cannot, or will not teach their children about this very delicate subject.

I also think that the school should teach this subject so the message can be consistent. I think children should begin this education early in life (4th Grade) when the urge to test, or experiment, is not present. Too many times we wait until the child is near puberty to teach them, and they test what they learn. If we wait until they are 10 or 12 years old too many things are going on in those young bodies, and young lives.

So what I am saying is, sex education should begin in the fourth grade, and develop as the child does.

The school should do the education, because if left up to parents only God knows what the young people will be taught.

If it were left up to parents like my father they may not get the complete message.

My sex talk as a young man was; "Boy you better keep that little worm in your paints, because if you make a baby you are going to have to go to work and take care of it." That was all I ever got out of him about sex! It was very effective for me because I did not want to, nor was I ready, to be a father.

We know that fathers are telling young girls that it is ok for them to have sex with their father. Mothers are telling young boys that it is ok to have sex with Mom. These are the extremes, but look at all the stuff in between. We cannot forget that teachers have always had sex with students, and some teachers think this is ok.

We are all human beings and in most cases, sex is sex. There should be some approved system for this process, and let's make America great and save our daughters. Too many young ladies get off to a bad start in life due to a lack of knowledge.

When a young lady has a child before the age of twenty, the chances are 50% that she will experience poverty. Some will experience it, and others will live in it!

People ask me about the church educating, and/or supporting some form of sex education. The church has a stand, and they should stay there: Abstinence until marriage!

The church should stay on abstinence, teach it and support. But it must be understood that abstinence only works for those young people who have decided to wait. Teaching abstinence provides support for that decision.

Statistics say that 50% of high school students have tried sex, and if it was a bad experience they join the ranks of abstinence, and will probably stay there. Those young people who have tried sex, and found it pleasurable, there is no turning back.

Most adults who tell the truth will agree!

The rest of us have to look at those who have chosen sex, and you know there is no turning back, at least for me. If you tell the truth, you too!

I feel it is better to have young people engage in sex, and do it safely, than to have them not knowing what they are doing, and ruining their lives with unwanted children too soon. Or, doing something unsafe and getting a disease that will be with them the rest of their lives. Or getting a disease that will take their life! I know I am fighting a losing battle on this one, but this is **my opinion**.

Opinion Number Ten

What Happened to the Bees?

For some time we have been hearing about the plight of the Honey Bees. How they have been dying off, how they leave the nest in search of food and nectar, and never return.

I was reading some research recently and found some interesting information. The bees have been flying around the world making honey for thousands of years, and in the last twenty years we have been unable to find them. Why?

The only thing that is new in their environment is computers, namely the cell phones. The research spoke of cell phones and their impact on the honey bee.

The honey bee uses the same kind of wave length that the cell phone uses.

If you look at the use of cell phones today, you too will be amazed. Everywhere you look someone is on the cell. People walk into walls, doors, other people, and into rivers. Yes, one guy walked into the river and had to be rescued!

Young people and adults are killed in automobile accidents while on the phone and not paying attention to what they are doing.

You can't drive a car and make phone calls at the same time! It does not work!

The death rate based on this fact is too evident!

Think about it: you make a call on your cell phone at the same time bee number 007 leaves the nest.

Bee number 007 has received information from one of his fellow bees to go and gather nectar at a certain location. But your call interferes with the signal, and bee number 007 heads out to sea.

In my opinion this makes more sense than anything I have heard to date. If anything could confuse the honey bee it would be the use of cell phones.

When you drive down the road and count the number of cell phones in use at any given time it is enough to confuse anyone, including the honey bee.

So, does the progress of man and the development of technology have such an impact on something as old and vital as the bee, and the making of honey, or the cross pollination of plants?

The honey bee impacts a lot of what man does, and his survival on this planet? What are we to do if this turns out to be the reason that the honey bee is disappearing?

I support this idea for the moment, because there is not another one that I am aware of. I will see what future research has to say on this issue.

Just to add to this issue, as the honey bee dies off, flies off, and stops making honey, think about the advance of the "African Killer Bee." They don't make honey, they kill people, and we don't know if the cell phone has a similar impact on them. Maybe it has no impact at all!

It is strange how the Bible says that man will become weaker and wiser, and then the end will come. Without the honey bee pollinating plants that we need, doing what they have been doing for centuries, and the evergrowing number of the killer bees, the end may not be sweet at all.

This issue interests me because of my background in zoology. When I attended Delhi University we studied the honey bee, and it was a very interesting topic.

My fellow Americans, this is not an issue we can, or should, take lightly!

Opinion Number Eleven

Healthy Food & the Poor Tax

There has been some talk about the "Sugar Tax": a tax that will charge people extra if they purchase sweet foods that are unhealthy.

This tax will be imposed on the "Poor" people of our society, because they are the ones that buy these cheap, unhealthy foods.

There has been a lot of talk about teaching "Poor" people how to eat healthy, and not spend money on these food products.

When we look at poor people, we see people who have no money to pay the high price of healthy foods. They also do not have transportation to go to the market to pay for high-priced healthy foods.

They instead walk to the corner store and pay for cheap, unhealthy foods like pop, chips, and processed meats full of salt and other chemicals.

In my Opinion the tax should be there to entice "Poor" people not to buy those unhealthy food products that cause so many health problems.

If you are poor, and insist on buying unhealthy food products, you should be willing to pay the tax.

If you are a business selling food to the poor, and are concerned about the health of your community, (and your customers) you will lower the price on healthy food.

Tax the unhealthy foods, and lower the prices on the healthy food. If this works, one will offset the other! The people will be spending the same amount of money, and eating much healthier.

Wegmans, Wal-Mart, and other outlets across the community would all buy into this concept, this would encourage the manufactures of unhealthy food products to change their ways.

The city could provide seeds for healthy food to be planted in these open lots across the city. Look at the First Lady of the United States: she has a garden in her back yard!

There is always the need for community education because we have people who have transportation to get to the market, money to purchase healthy foods, and still they buy unhealthy products.

These are the ones who need the education, and are able to pay the tax if they refuse to change. The tax is part of the education...the stick, if you will! I know from working in the community for many years you have to get people's attention before they will allow you to educate them.

All over NY state people are complaining about the sugar tax. If the tax was not there people would not be upset, and the opportunity to educate would not be present.

Now they will hear you when you tell them that a bottle of pop has too much sugar in it, and that they should not buy it.

In the Bible the farmer gathered his harvest and allowed the poor to get the leftovers before he prepared the ground for another season.

That principle could work today. In upstate NY there are farmers who leave a lot of food in the fields to just go bad. If the city and the schools would provide the transportation to take poor people out to the farms, this food would not be wasted.

There are many things this country could do to assist the poor if they could find the will.

OPINION NUMBER TWELVE

<u>The Bernie Maddox Story</u>

In 2008 the American economy hit rock bottom, and all the crooked, underhanded money schemes were exposed. One of them that was uncovered was where a man named Maddox was taking people's money and running a "hook and hide."

In this "hook and hide" people were told that they could invest one dollar, and when they get it back they would receive one dollar and 35 cents.

The hooker would spend the money any way he wanted because when he got the next victim he would use some of that money to pay the first one.

At first many people were getting a 35% return. The same thing happened that always happens. The "hooker" overspends all that easy money and the funds start to run low. It could have gone on if the market did not try to right itself, and it all went tumbling down.

When it was exposed 50 Billion dollars had been hooked, and hidden. A lot was spent too!

In my Opinion all of the people who got caught in this one was because of their GREED. Greed is a disease that has no cure, nor treatment. Once you are infected, you are doomed for the rest of your life.

Mr. Maddox took a lot of people, some of whom were experienced investors, and they were all greedy, and I have no sympathy for them.

First they all knew that there was no such thing as a 35% return on your money; 20% if the market is doing very well, but 35% is unheard of, and this is what Maddox promised these people.

Many of them were receiving 35% return on their investments at first, and the scheme may have continued if the American economy did not collapse.

Mr. Maddox was taking one person's money and paying off the last one. Stealing from Peter to pay Paul (and taking the next investor's money to pay Peter and on down the line). There were people waiting in line to get into the Maddox scheme.

He and his family were living the good life and so were some of the first investors. Then the bubble burst, and all came tumbling down. All of the investors were angry with Maddox, the federal agents were after Maddox, and people were losing their homes and their money.

It was their GREED!

They all bought into the lie that they could get 35% return on their money. I don't blame Maddox for their losses, I blame their greed.

Then once it was all said and done Mr. Maddox was sentenced to 250 years in prison. The man is 70 years old now, why would they do such a stupid thing?

I guess some of the investors got what they deserved when they lost their money, and their homes.

Many Americans are losing their life savings, and their life's earning with many of these companies going out of business, and the workers go home with nothing.

The CEOs of these companies are walking away with millions, and the workers who have given these companies their lives are getting nothing. Some of them are losing their homes, and the federal government and their agents are doing nothing.

Somebody ought to arrest those CEOs and take away their millions and give it to the workers that have been ripped off. Instead they are selling off Maddox's belongings and giving the money to some of his so-called victims. They are just as much the blame for their condition as Maddox.

Those American workers who lost homes (and more) as a result of the CEOs doing the same thing that Maddox did should be compensated.

Those workers were not being greedy like the Maddox partners were.

Where is the JUSTICE America?

OPINION NUMBER THIRTEEN

Tiger Woods

It has taken four months for Tiger Woods to come out of hiding after he got caught with several other women. The boy had me fooled; I never saw that in Tiger!

I was convinced that he was a clean cut young man who learned to play golf when he was very young. His body developed into a golfing machine. He still has it, and when he gets his head back on he will do the same thing that OJ did. Find him another White girl to take his money. They should take it all! (Poor thing!)

Of course the media is having a field day with this issue. This is another opportunity for America to degrade one of its Black success stories.

Tiger Woods has done what many other American men have done, that is having an affair outside of his marriage. The White president did it, revered sports figures have done it, and governors of states have done it. Some of the men have been caught with other men. All of them have to pay a price when they get caught.

All these months the media has been after him to come out with a statement, and an apology. I am sure that he has apologized to his wife a thousand times, and to those close to him. These are the ones who have to deal with that mistake.

In my OPINION, he does not owe the world or America a damn thing! Tiger Woods did not become the person that he is because of his lifestyle with women, nor his ability to speak in public. He became famous because he can hit a golf ball better than anyone in the world.

All the sponsors who paid Tiger Woods to use his name and his ability as a golfer to make money earned more money than Tiger. These companies made money off of Tiger and when he made the same mistake that others have made they pulled their support. So when Tiger gets back on the course, they are going to have to pay double to endorse him again.

All these women who have been damaged by their relationship with Tiger will now receive their 15 minutes of fame, and they may make a little money. I am very sorry that all of them were White women. This only shows what Tiger likes (poor thing).

His wife is no better than those other women, because she has renegotiated her contract with Tiger so when she leaves (and she will leave) she will leave with a lot more of his money.

It seems strange for people to negotiate an agreement as to what will take place in case of divorce, and then at the end of the relationship the rules change. I had never heard of that until this case. She was supposed to get several million dollars under certain conditions of the divorce. When the courts changed the rules she walked away with 300 million.

Where is the justice for the Black man?

He just needs to get out there on the course and do what he does better than anyone in the world: play golf. Take out all his frustrations on that little white ball. Win, win, win, and all will be ok for him, and his.

I don't care if he thinks he is Black or anything else he claims. I claim the Black in him he got from his father, and you can claim what you want.

I know what all of White America thinks of him, and the White golfers hope he never comes back on the course. Then maybe some of them can win a game or two. But if Tiger is out there, they are scared that he will be within a few strokes to taking it all again.

OPINION NUMBER FOURTEEN

<u>Pants on the Ground</u>

Over the years I have observed several things that young people did that aggravated me to no end. First, it was young women getting pregnant at a very young age (14-15-16 years of age) that drove me crazy. I ask God to help me, and I prayed my way through it. After all, Mary had Jesus when she was 15 years old.

Next was the men with ear rings, first in one ear, and then in two. That too drove me crazy, and I prayed my way through that one too.

The football players, the movie stars, and homosexual all had good reasons for wearing ear rings. Young mothers were putting these ear rings in their young son's ears at very young ages.

Now I am in the process of praying my way through the young men and their pants hanging down on the ground with a belt on, and you can see half of their ass.

It began in the eighties with young men sagging: that is wearing their pants below their waist about half way covering their butts, and you could see their naked ass.

God must have touched them, and then they started wearing the pants below their butts, and their shorts above their navel, or above the waist.

This has been going on for a long time now, and most of us older men thought it was a passing fad, but it has not passed. These kinds of things have happened before in this American society, but they go away after a few years.

All the young Black entertainers are wearing them that way. They are advertised on TV that way, and even the White boys are wearing them that way.

Mr. Willie Lynch said over five hundred years ago, once we were put on the path of self-hatred, and self-destruction, we would find ways to perpetuate it on our own.

In my OPINION, we have to decide if this is just a fad? When I question young men about why they wear their pants hanging down on the ground, with their asses showing, they say" we wear them that way because we can! We wear them that way because we know you hate it, and you can do nothing about it! It is the style."

Some young men told me the clothes hanging off them means they are shading the White man's conditioning; preparing themselves for the future.

For older men like me they say to just get over it. We must decide if it has any substance: does it really mean anything, or should we just let it pass.

"Pants on the ground, Pants on the ground,
 walking around looking like a fool, with your pants on the ground."
"Hat turned around, with your pants on the ground,
 showing your shorts, with your pants on the ground.
 Looking like a fool with your pants on the ground."

I saw some guy on TV with this poem, I thought it was great.

So I say to adults across the United States: feel sorry for them fools with their pants hanging down, but don't get too overly concerned because it has no substance. It makes no sense!

There is an issue with Black men taking their rightful place in this society, but that is another issue. If the young men are angry with us for not teaching them how to be men in America (the Black father issue) let's just pray that they will pull up their pants one day, and get them off the ground.

OPINION NUMBER FIFTEEN

The Death Penalty

Another one of the most talked about issues in America is the use of the death penalty. Should we use it, do we have the right to use it?

As I have stated many times though all of my writing is how I was taught to use the Bible. My father said that the answer to all of Man's questions is in the Bible. So let's go there first.

I would strongly recommend that you read the entire chapter of Numbers 35 to get the full picture of this point.

Numbers 35:16: *And if he smite him with an instrument of iron, so that he die, he is a murderer: the murderer shall surely be put to death.*

Verse 17 says: *If he throw a stone and kills someone, he is a murderer, and the murderer shall be put to death, surely!*

Verse 18 says: *If he kills him with a wood weapon, the murderer shall surely be put to death.*

Verse 20 says: *If he kills him after lying in wait for him to pass, or* (verse 21) *kills him in enmity, or anger, strike him with his hand and he die, he is a murderer, and the murderer shall surely be put to death.*

Verses 22 and 23, address accidental death; in these cases the congregation shall judge between the slayer and the dead man's family.

Verse 31 says: *Ye shall take no satisfaction for the life of the murderer, which is guilty of death: but he shall be surely put to death.*

Verses 33 and 34 read: *"So ye shall not **POLLUTE** the land wherein you are: for blood it defileth the land: and the land cannot be cleansed of the blood that is shed therein, but by the blood of him that shed it.Defile not therefore the land which ye shall inhabit, wherein I dwell: for I the Lord dwell among the children of Israel.*

Genesis 9:6 says: *Whosoever sheddeth man's blood, by man shall his blood be shed: for in the image of God made He man.*

There has been murder since the beginning of time, and there will always be murder. The death penalty was never intended to stop people from killing one another. It was designed to get rid of the murderer, the killer, and not pollute the land in which we live.

It is strange how many Americans claim they believe in the Bible, preachers who claim they teach from the Bible can use it to support what they want, and make excuses when it does not support what they want.

I have heard all the reasons why people say they don't support the death penalty, but **In My Opinion** it is all fluff! You can believe what you please, but don't say what the Bible say until you read it.

The mental state of the murderer is of no consequence; he or she must surely be put to death. If we as a society do not put the murderer to death we pollute the land in which we live, plain and simple. I have the Bible to support my claim. What do you have?

The land we live on in America is polluted because our prisons are full of murderers who we have given a life sentence! That is why we have no room in prison for the rapist and the robber, because the jail cells are occupied by murderers.

The rapist and the robber continue to rape and rob because we have no place to put them. They continue to take what does not belong to them, sometimes killing in the process.

The rapist continues to ruin people's lives, mess up the young girls lives before they can become young ladies, and because the prisons are full of murderers they remain among us committing crimes, polluting the land, and our society.

We in America spend countless dollars feeding and caring for the murderer because we gave him (or her) life, when we should have given them death so that we can clean our land of all this pollution.

Remember that Jesus said He did not come to change, but to fulfill.

Jesus did not say the woman should not be stoned; He said you cast the first stone! None of us can cast the stone because we are all guilty of so much wrong.

But the murderer most be put to death when he or she has had a fair trial and found guilty by their peers.

Remember the Bible says only the blood of them that shed blood will cleanse the land. The murderer should surely be put to death!

OPINION NUMBER SIXTEEN

Why is everyone so Angry?

Everywhere you go these days everyone is so angry. Why? When you go to the store to purchase goods the cashier is angry, and will let you know he or she does not want to be there.

If you go to the Doctor's office the receptionist will let you know in words or deeds that they do not want to be there, and they are angry about something.

Young people are angry. Old people are angry. Everybody is upset about something. And the look they give you is ominous. Why?

I am sure that you have asked yourself this question many times as you go about your day. I know I have!

I work at a medical building where people come for medical care. People come in the door angry and ready for a fight.

They want to fight the people who are going to provide care for them. They want to fight with the people who are going to be giving them medications, and sticking them with needles. Why?

I see people coming in for care and start "cussing" the nurse out. They "cuss" out the doctor and they are the ones that are ill. I wonder if they are aware that the same people they are "cussing" out are the same people who will be providing them the medication that can cure, or kill.

In my opinion people are angry, first, because they do not have all the money they think they need. Many women are angry because they do not have a man to call their own. In many instances they are sharing with someone else.

There are statistics that say 75% of American women don't have a man. The only thing I say to that is ladies you set your standards too high. The man most of you are looking for does not exist.

I heard a young lady say," I don't want to control my man, I just want him to do like I say!"

Ladies, to us men, they both are the same!

The men you meet are angry because they can't do the things they used to, and are angry because they can't. They try and fail, and then blame everybody else because he is no longer the man he used to be! Sounds crazy, but true!

The sad part about all of this is that no one is willing to admit this is a fact! So they always show you that anger, and you don't think about the real reasons.

Young girls are angry because their fathers left and they never receive the love of a man as children. When they become young women all the men want is sex, and somebody to abuse.

They never received the love from a man like their father, or their brother. These young ladies need a male relative to tell them they are loved.

The first time they hear a man saying he loves them is when he is trying to get them out of their clothes.

They are angry because their mothers don't, or can't, teach them how to be real women. Their mothers are in the club with them competing for the young men, trying to prove they are something they are not; much like the men!

Everybody is looking for something they think is missing. When they can't find it they blame someone else, and are angry about it.

The young men are angry because their father left and there was no one to teach him how to be a man, and how to treat women. So he treats them badly, and with no respect. He was raised by his mother who tried to teach him how to be a man, and unknowingly she was teaching him how to be the man she wanted, and does not have. The young man is very confused.

He hears one thing in the barbershop, and he hears another when his mother trains him at home.

Many people are angry because they are overweight, and they continue to eat because they are angry. (P.S. That will never assist in getting the weight off!)

Then there is that ever present racism. Everywhere we go in today's society there is that thing that should have gone away long ago.

We all have to deal with it because it is always there! It serves no purpose in today's society. There is no reason for it in the 21st century. It might have served a purpose 200 years ago to assist in maintaining the institution of slavery but it only makes people look bad, and keeps them angry for nothing today.

The primary problem with racism is that we as Americans are afraid to simply talk about it. We as a people need to have the conversation. Let's just talk it out America!

OPINION NUMBER SEVENTEEN

<u>Trayvon Martin & George Zimmerman</u>

All America has heard about this case because it is so recent. It is much like many others of its kind in America.

My fellow Americans RACE is in everything we do in America. We first need to stop talking about entering race into any situation we deal with in this country. It is always there, always.

This country was built on race. Stop fighting that America, it is our history!

I would have loved to have been a fly on the wall in that jury room as those five White women, and one Latino woman deliberated this case. You can never understand what could have gone on in that room unless you have gone through it yourself. I have been part of a jury on a murder case!

Here is my opinion. There was enough evidence presented in that case for those women to rule any way they wanted to and feel good about it. All they had to do was to pick one, guilty or not!

The thing they had to deliberate was who was going to move out of Sanford, Florida.

If they had convicted him they would have had to move out of Sanford. The White folk in Sanford would have run them out of town. If they let him go he and his family would have to move out of Sanford.

Being born and raised in Sanford I knew the attitude of that community. The people have changed, but the attitudes are the same. I told my wife from the start of this whole thing that he would be set free!

The jury was five White women and one Latino woman ruling on a racially charged case like this. These women have to live in that small town after all this was done. So they had to decide if they and their families were going to move out of town, or was George Z. and his family going to move. They made the right choice.

I work in a facility of about 200 employees, and we see 500 patients a day. The entire time of the trial not a word was uttered by White folks pertaining to the trial. Normally the staff in that building talked about every news item that arose, but not this one! The same thing happened with the OJ Simpson trial.

The only conversation (regarding the trial) was between Whites with Whites, and Blacks with Blacks.

This is the problem with RACE in America. No one wants to talk about it. That is what must happen if we are going to get better about managing this issue, and manage it we must!

It appears to me that the law was followed, but justice was not done!

The best comment I heard was by the daughter of Dr. Martin Luther King. When she said it I heard her father saying it. The question was what would her father be during in this situation? She said "He would be encouraging orderly discourse." That is beautiful! I could hear his voice when she said it. I will always respect her for that statement. So well put. So well put!

This book is an attempt to allow you to get to know me better. I hope that sharing my retirement speech with you will assist in that effort.

Freddie Caldwell's Closing Remarks

Good Evening!

First, I would like to introduce to you my wife Peggy Caldwell who has worked very hard to make this event a success.

Thank you Peggy, you did a great job!

Secondly, I would like to thank the team that worked with Peggy, a team she put together and they planned all this for us tonight.

It is not an easy task to get people together at the same time, and same place, for the same purpose. Thank you so much!

Next I want to thank all of you for coming out and assisting Peggy and me to begin this transition from the work world to the world of retirement. There are those who told me they wanted to be here with me, but others things were more important: like weddings, vacations, and out of town business.

Each of you has contributed in some way to where I am at this stage in my life, and I thank you for the opportunity to learn from you. To work with you on the many projects we have completed, and the ones we did not complete. As the young people say: "It's all good."

I was born in Sanford, Florida August 6, 1946. I went to Hopper Elementary School and graduated from Crooms High School on June 7, 1965. On July 20, 1965 I was employed at Rochester General Hospital-Westside Division. I know that most of you may have never heard of RGH Westside Division, but there was such a place.

In 1966 the Westside Division moved over to Rochester General Hospital Northside Division. There are a few people in Rochester who still refer to RGH as "Northside."

In June of 1966 I was drafted into the US Army and spent three months at Fort Monroe, Virginia, and 19 months in Baumholder, Germany.

In 1968 I returned to RGH, and all totaled I worked 40 years at RGH. Thirty two years of that was in the Charles O. Sailor Animal Research Laboratory, in the department of Surgery and Education.

In the early 1990's RGH started the process of cross-training, and I cross-trained in the Human Resources Department-Education Division where I became the Director of Cultural Diversity Initiatives, and support staff to the Practical Nursing school where I connected nursing students with community supports that provided assistance as they completed their schooling.

During those 40 years 27 of them I spent volunteering with and for Action for a Better Community Inc. I started volunteering at ABC in 1975.

When I retired from RGH I was asked to join the staff at ABC as Deputy Director for Community Services Division where I have come to know so many of you present tonight. I have learned many things from you, and I hope that some of you may have learned some things from me as well. Fair exchange does no harm to anyone!

The best mentors of my life were my farther Denver C. Caldwell, who believed that everything has a place, and everything should be in its place. He was hard, and strict, in teaching that lesson.

Daddy Melvin McCray, another life mentor, taught me about people: how some are good and some are not, but you have to love them all. He was a great teacher, and stayed on one subject until you got it.

James Mamba McCuller, former Executive Director of ABC taught us to "plan your work, and then work your plan." He called it the 5 P's (Proper Planning Prevents Poor Performance). You have to get your plan off the drawing board if you are ever going to know if it will fail or succeed.

"Good Better Best, Never let it Rest, until your Good gets Better, and your Better becomes your Best."

My friend and former boss James H. Norman, who taught me grace and poise under pressure. There have been times when I would go into his office with what I perceived as a problem, and I thought there were two or three choices of solutions, but when I left his office I had five or six choices of solutions and two of mine got eliminated! Great teacher and support is James H. Norman. Thank you James!

Lastly my friend and pastor, Rev. James Cherry, who taught me in a special way the understanding that "Jesus is Alive," and always willing to help in time of need.

So here we are my wife and I, at the crossroads of work and retirement, and everybody wants to know what I am going to do.

- I am going to love my wife, and get to know her in a new way. When I leave work I go home to her, she always makes me laugh. Those of you who know me well know that I love to laugh.
- James Norman tells me that the more golf balls you hit, the better you get at hitting them, so I plan to hit a lot of golf balls.

- I want to try my hand a public speaking because I think I have a story to tell about HIV and AIDS, a very ugly disease that we can take care of if people listen, and do the right things.

I also can talk about Poverty (another ugly monster in our midst) that many do not understand. I need to tell those in Poverty that they need not suffer as much as they do because there are people and organizations willing to help them through any crisis, and Poverty need not last a lifetime.

As a nation, until we all sit down and have an in-depth conversation on the issue of RACE this nation will never become what it is capable of becoming.

To me this is retirement, because I am committed to making my life better by helping others make theirs better. Now it will be on my time schedule.

I want all of us to know that we must work to make the lives of the UN's in our society better.

The UN's:

The Under-Counted.

The Under-Represented.

The UN-Insured.

The UN-Educated.

The UN-Trusting.

The UN-Employed.

The Under-Served.

The UN-Saved (Rev. Cherry).

The UN-Protected.

The UN-Healthy.

The UN-Tested (Jerald & Naimah).

The Under-Fed.

The UN-Transported.

The UN-Willing to do for themselves.

The Under-Paid.

The UN-Hopeful.

The UN-Born.

So if anyone should ever write my life story, for whatever reason there might be, Rochester, New York and Sanford, Florida, you will be there between each line of pain and glory, because you are the best thing that ever happened to me!